Cambridge Elements

Elements in Creativity and Imagination
edited by
Anna Abraham
University of Georgia, USA

DESIGN THINKING AND OTHER APPROACHES

How Different Disciplines See, Think and Act

Nathan Crilly
University of Cambridge

CAMBRIDGE
UNIVERSITY PRESS

Shaftesbury Road, Cambridge CB2 8EA, United Kingdom

One Liberty Plaza, 20th Floor, New York, NY 10006, USA

477 Williamstown Road, Port Melbourne, VIC 3207, Australia

314–321, 3rd Floor, Plot 3, Splendor Forum, Jasola District Centre, New Delhi – 110025, India

103 Penang Road, #05–06/07, Visioncrest Commercial, Singapore 238467

Cambridge University Press is part of Cambridge University Press & Assessment, a department of the University of Cambridge.

We share the University's mission to contribute to society through the pursuit of education, learning and research at the highest international levels of excellence.

www.cambridge.org
Information on this title: www.cambridge.org/9781009498678

DOI: 10.1017/9781009498685

First published 2024

A catalogue record for this publication is available from the British Library.

ISBN 978-1-009-49867-8 Hardback
ISBN 978-1-009-49866-1 Paperback
ISSN 2752-3950 (online)
ISSN 2752-3942 (print)

The data underlying this work are provided in additional resources: www.cambridge.org/Crilly

Design Thinking and Other Approaches

How Different Disciplines See, Think and Act

Elements in Creativity and Imagination

DOI: 10.1017/9781009498685
First published online: June 2024

Nathan Crilly
University of Cambridge
Author for correspondence: Nathan Crilly, nc266@cam.ac.uk

Abstract: Efforts to promote creativity often centre on encouraging people to engage in 'design thinking', 'systems thinking' and 'entrepreneurial thinking'. These different approaches are most often defined, taught and applied in mutual isolation, which has obscured what distinguishes them from each other, what they have in common and how they might be combined. These three approaches are also most often described in isolation from the approaches that characterise other disciplines, all of which are relevant to how problems are identified, framed and solved. These other approaches include 'computational thinking', 'engineering thinking', 'scientific thinking', 'evolutionary thinking', 'mathematical thinking', 'statistical thinking', 'geographical thinking', 'historical thinking', 'anthropological thinking' and many more. Examining these approaches as a set allows each of them to be better understood, and also reveals the connections and contrasts between them. Such comparisons provide the foundation for a more coordinated project to represent how different disciplinary approaches contribute to creative work.

Keywords: design thinking, systems thinking, entrepreneurial thinking, computational thinking, mathematical thinking

ISBNs: 9781009498678 (HB), 9781009498661 (PB), 9781009498685 (OC)
ISSNs: 2752-3950 (online), 2752-3942 (print)

Contents

Online appendices are available at
www.cambridge.org/Crilly

1 Considering Disciplinary Approaches

A designer, an ecologist and an entrepreneur walk into a bar . . .

A joke that starts like this would later develop in ways that illustrate the different approaches the three protagonists take to the world around them. The joke and its punchline (normally at the expense of whoever is third in the list) hinge on these distinctive differences being understood by the audience. So, what sort of differences would be relevant to our three friends? Perhaps the designer sees everything as a creative challenge; perhaps the ecologist sees everything as a system of interacting parts; perhaps the entrepreneur sees everything as a match between changing opportunities and changing resources. Perhaps, and perhaps a joke of some sort can be structured around these supposed differences in outlook or mindset. However, note that for the joke to work, we must all implicitly understand that these individuals each have an approach that will influence not just their professional activities, but also their orientation to whatever scenario they are about to encounter in the bar they are walking into.

Is that true? Do practitioners from individual disciplines have distinctive approaches at such a general level? What kind of thing are these approaches, what are they composed of and how are they related to each other? Are they relevant even beyond the bounds of their originating disciplines? Can people be effectively trained in those 'disciplinary approaches' and then apply those approaches to other contexts? How would such people identify the approaches of most interest to them, either individually or in combination? These are the sorts of questions that I will address in this work, not for the purposes of joke construction – as entertaining as that might be – but to inform how we think about disciplinary approaches in general. This is important because these approaches are central to many of the decisions that we make within and across disciplines, including decisions about collaboration, education and training.

Many disciplines have already conducted and reported significant work in their efforts to characterise the distinctive features of their own approaches. For example, referring to our three friends again, the training and professional experiences they each have might mean they are skilled in or inclined toward what is sometimes called 'design thinking' (e.g. Kimbell, 2011), 'systems thinking' (e.g. M. C. Jackson, 2003) or 'entrepreneurial thinking' (e.g. Krueger, 2007). Each of these approaches has been promoted as important to the disciplines that they are most closely associated with, but also to many other domains and applications. In recent years, this has been especially true for management practices (e.g. Gharajedaghi, 2011; Liedtka & Ogilvie, 2011; McGrath & MacMillan, 2000), and therefore management education (e.g. see Dunne & Martin, 2006; Glen et al., 2014; Peschl et al., 2021; Seiler & Kowalsky, 2011).

Consequently, each of these approaches has been reported across the general business press, including in publications such as *BusinessWeek*, *Fast Company*, *Forbes*, *Fortune*, *Harvard Business Review* and the *Financial Times*.[1] These approaches have also been advocated by many local and national governments (e.g. Kavanagh, 2021; Liedtka et al., 2020; UK Government Office for Science, 2022), and also by inter-governmental organisations such as the United Nations, the World Bank and the World Health Organization (de Savigny & Taghreed, 2009; United Nations Development Programme, 2017; Valerio et al., 2014).[2] In all cases, these forms of thinking are promoted for their potential to encourage new perspectives, expand imagination and boost creativity.

Whilst design thinking, systems thinking and entrepreneurial thinking might have received the most attention from those promoting problem finding, problem framing and problem solving, these are not the only approaches that are relevant to how people understand, manage and change the world around them. If our joke instead started with a computer scientist, an engineer and a statistician walking into the same bar, then the generally applicable approaches they each would be expected to take might be referred to as 'computational thinking' (e.g. Wing, 2006), 'engineering thinking' (e.g. Waks et al., 2011) and 'statistical thinking' (e.g. Chance, 2002). Across a wide range of literatures, many such disciplinary approaches have been defined, debated, promoted, criticised and defended. A non-exhaustive list would include those already mentioned but also many other approaches, which can be usefully (but only approximately) grouped under conventional disciplinary categories:

- *The professions* – design thinking, entrepreneurial thinking and engineering thinking (all cited above), technological thinking (e.g. Gorman, 2006), architectural thinking (e.g. Frascari, 2009), systems-architectural thinking (e.g. Aier et al., 2015), policy thinking (Geva-May, 2005) and thinking like a doctor (e.g. Loftus, 2018), nurse (e.g. Tanner, 2006) or lawyer (e.g. Rapoport, 2002).
- *The sciences* – systems thinking, computational thinking and statistical thinking (all cited above), mathematical thinking (e.g. Burton, 1984), scientific thinking (e.g. Noll, 1935), physics thinking (e.g. Sayre & Irving, 2015), chemical thinking (e.g. Sevian & Talanquer, 2014), evolutionary thinking (e.g. Novick & Catley, 2016) and data-scientific thinking (e.g. Cao, 2018; Gould, 2021).

---

[1] For example, for design thinking, see work by Higgins (2020), Nussbaum (2004) and Speicher et al. (2022); for systems thinking see work by Praslova (2023) and Tank (2020); for entrepreneurial thinking, see work by Crudo (2020) and Hoberman (2015).

[2] More generally, design thinking has been promoted as the means by which governments or democratic systems could be developed (Saward, 2021).

- *The social sciences* – geographical thinking (e.g. P. Jackson, 2006), sociological thinking (e.g. Ruggiero, 1996), anthropological thinking (e.g. Tett, 2021, pp. xiv–xv) and economic thinking (e.g. Mankiw & Taylor, 2014, pp. 3–29).
- *The arts and humanities* – historical thinking (e.g. Andrews & Burke, 2007), craft thinking (e.g. Ings, 2015), literary thinking (e.g. Langer, 1998) and artistic thinking (e.g. Sullivan, 2001).

Despite all the work that has been done to describe many specific disciplinary approaches, they have not previously been drawn together for comparison and integration, which is what I aim to do here. But why draw them together at all? If these disciplines are independently going about the work of describing what constitutes their distinctive approaches, why not just leave them to it? Well, one reason is that if these approaches are distinctive to each discipline, then they are at least implicitly distinctive in relation to something else, such as other disciplines. For example, the individual approaches of our three friends entering the bar – whatever disciplines they are now drawn from – would, we hope, become better defined in contrast to each other as the joke unfolds: there is clarity in comparison.

Another reason to draw the approaches together is that disciplinary divisions are often rather arbitrary and can mask the similarities and overlaps between what different groups of people are doing and how they are doing it. Just as the disciplines are related to each other in interesting ways, so are their approaches. Because of this, anyone wanting to learn or apply a specific disciplinary approach (such as design thinking) would benefit from understanding how it relates to any approaches they are already familiar with, given their own disciplinary background. They would also benefit from understanding how it relates to other contrasting or complementary approaches, approaches that they might also want to discover. However, such understanding might be hard to arrive at because descriptions of these approaches are scattered through a large and confusing set of literatures that are barely connected by references that cut across disciplines. Furthermore, the courses that teach the approaches largely do so in mutual isolation (e.g. for reviews of design thinking syllabi, see Wiesche et al., 2018; Wrigley et al., 2018; Wrigley & Straker, 2017). The result is that individual disciplinary approaches are difficult to locate, and the relations between them are difficult to establish.

Fragmentation of the literatures, courses and communities related to disciplinary approaches acts as a barrier to innovation. For example, referring to the introduction of design thinking into management, Boland and Collopy (2004) explained that '[t]he more ways of thinking we have available to us, the better our problem-solving outcomes can be' (p. 11). However, as we have seen, design thinking is only one of many 'ways of thinking' that we might wish to select and implement. If someone from management or elsewhere became interested in design thinking, how would they identify other approaches that might also be complementary, whether systems thinking, entrepreneurial thinking or something else? Alternatively, if someone recognised that empathising with users and customers was a valuable feature of both design thinking and entrepreneurial thinking, how would they become aware of the related features of anthropological thinking and economic thinking? Finally, if someone found that the application of systems thinking was a valuable way of expanding their understanding of the situations they were trying to intervene in, how would they come to recognise that evolutionary thinking and geographical thinking might also be useful for this? At present, the answer to all these questions would unfortunately be, 'with great difficulty!'

To address the problem of fragmentation, I here survey many of the disciplinary 'thinking' projects that have been conducted and are ongoing. This allows me to draw out the connections and contrasts between the projects, between the approaches they have defined, and between the components that they have used to build those definitions. To achieve this, I first offer a discussion of terminology and scope to allow disciplinary approaches to be described more clearly, both at the level of the individual disciplines and at the level of a more abstract unifying concept. I then focus on the overall descriptions of disciplinary approaches, investigating what kinds of things these approaches are, the extent to which they are agreed on and the motivations for describing them. This sets the context for presenting a collection of disciplinary approaches and the components they are made up of, tabulated for convenient comparison, both within and across disciplines. I then shift focus from individual descriptions of disciplinary approaches to the ways in which they overlap, and the gaps between them. I assess what the approaches are defined in contrast to, the extent to which they are discipline-specific, the ways in which they might be transferred to other contexts, and how sub-disciplines and inter-disciplines are handled. All this motivates calls for a more coordinated cross-cutting project to define disciplinary approaches. These calls are supported by a sketch of the limited kinds of comparison and consolidation that are possible at present, and suggestions for the kinds of work required to achieve greater coordination in future.

Overall, this work is aimed at supporting those who want to research, teach, learn or apply any particular disciplinary approach to also identify the complementary or contrasting approaches that other disciplines have to offer.[3]

---

[3] For example, the design research community have for many years talked about 'designerly ways of knowing' (Cross, 1982), but this is just one specific form of 'disciplinary ways of knowing' (Messer-Davidow et al., 1993).

More ambitiously, I also intend to stimulate interest in the general concept of disciplinary approaches, rather than just the specific approaches that have seemingly dominated people's attention so far. I hope that is useful, even if it is not very funny.

2 Establishing Terminology and Scope

As we'll see, it is characteristic of the projects that define disciplinary approaches that the same words are used to mean different things, and that different things are meant by the same words. These observations can be made not just across disciplines but also within them. While I aim to remain faithful to the intended meanings of the authors I cite, adhering to their terminology too closely would sometimes lead to a proliferation of distracting terms. Because a certain consistency is required here, I have tried to standardise the language used and apply that language across disciplines and authors, even if this sometimes requires deviating from the original terms. In addition, because we will be looking across multiple disciplines, connecting and comparing different bodies of work, it is necessary to have some new terminology for concepts that are more general than those that are required when only focussing on any single discipline. For example, the term 'disciplinary approach' is only necessary if one is interested in *the type of thing* that design thinking, systems thinking and entrepreneurial thinking are.

There are five key terms to focus on here:

- *Disciplines* – I'll use the terms 'disciplines' and 'disciplinary' to refer to forms of coordination and control related to knowledge and behaviour. This is very broad, but disciplines are most often exemplified by academic subjects (e.g. mathematics, history) and professional practices (e.g. design, entrepreneurship). In many cases, the boundaries between such subjects and practices are blurred, because those working within academic subjects are expert practitioners (e.g. mathematicians, historians), and professional practices are studied and taught academically (e.g. design research and entrepreneurship training).[4]
- *Approaches* – I'll use the general term 'approaches' to refer to how practitioners in a particular discipline see the world, orient toward it and act upon it. This includes how they think, but also what they think about, what they know, what skills they have, what they are inclined to do and the personal qualities they exhibit. This use of 'approach' is intended to be inclusive of terms like

---

[4] See Sections 6.2, 6.3 and 6.4 for a much more detailed discussion of disciplines, including consideration of sub-disciplines and inter-disciplines, and an examination of whether something like systems thinking should be regarded as a specific disciplinary approach or a general higher-order thinking skill.

disciplinary 'thinking', 'mindset' and 'habits of mind', without being restricted to only cognitive abilities or characteristics.

- *Components* – I'll use the term 'components' to refer to the different parts or ingredients that make up any disciplinary approach (e.g. a collection of different ways of thinking or different things to pay attention to). Lists of such components are often central to descriptions of what characterises the approaches. These lists are typically unstructured, but can also be presented in order of importance, arranged in a hierarchy or presented in some other diagrammatic form. Either way, components are here taken to collectively describe, define or represent the disciplinary approach. For example, some components of the disciplinary approach called 'design thinking' might include empathy, visualisation and creativity.

- *Variants* – I'll use the term 'variants' to refer to the different proposals that have been made for any particular discipline's approach. These variants are typically proposed by different authors focussing on the same discipline, and they are typically distinguished from each other by their differing lists of components. For example, in discussions of design thinking, two different authors (or sets of authors) might each propose their own variant of design thinking, with one of those variants emphasising empathy, and the other not.

- *Projects* – I'll use the term 'projects' to refer to the collected attempts that have been made to define specific disciplinary approaches, possibly including numerous variants. For example, I'll refer to the distributed efforts to define 'design thinking' as though they are a single project, even if the authors and communities engaged in this work have not seen it as such. To be clear, I am retrospectively grouping different authors' work together and referring to those works as a single project, without meaning to imply that there was necessarily a well-coordinated effort toward a common goal.[5] This has the benefit of allowing related literatures to be grouped together and easily referred to for comparison and analysis.

See Figure 1 for an illustration of how these terms relate to each other and are combined.

While projects aiming to describe individual disciplinary approaches need not use any of the terms I have defined here, there is one term that is nearly ubiquitous, and which also requires some care: *'thinking'*.[6] Many authors append that word to a (modified) discipline name to label a disciplinary

---

[5] It is a project in the same way we could talk of 'the project of science', even though not all scientist (across scientific disciplines) are acting in a coordinated manner (e.g. see Schroyer, 1984, p. 720; Tollefsen, 2020, p. 279).

[6] See Athreya and Mouza's (2017) work for a review of definitions of thinking (§3.1) and a discussion of types of thinking (§3.2).

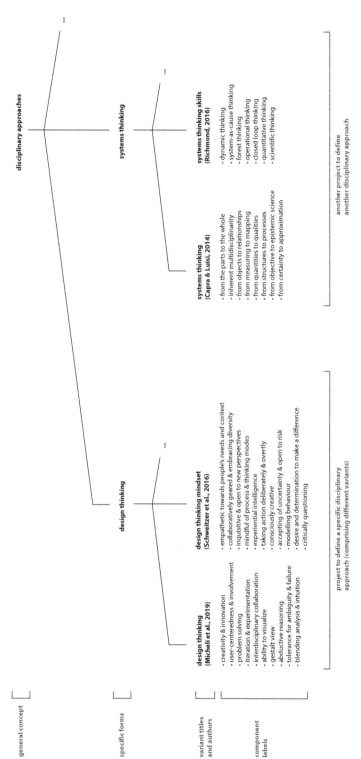

Figure 1 Diagram showing how the main concepts used in this work are related and combined. Starting at the top, there is a general concept of disciplinary approaches, which design thinking and systems thinking (etc.) are specific forms of. Each form of disciplinary approach is given different titles by different authors, and each author also typically lists a set of components that collectively make up the variant being described. These variants collectively make up the project that the discipline is undertaking to describe its approach.

approach, such as 'design thinking' or 'mathematical thinking'. This is the case even if those authors are not necessarily only discussing thinking, strictly considered (we'll return to this later). So, when I use terms like 'design thinking' and 'mathematical thinking', I am referring to the labels commonly applied to particular disciplinary approaches, rather than making a claim about the cognitive basis of that approach. Also, for consistency, I generally refer to specific disciplinary approaches in the form of '[discipline] thinking', such as 'geographical thinking' and 'anthropological thinking', even if some authors use alternative forms, such as 'thinking geographically' (P. Jackson, 2006) and 'think like an anthropologist' (Engelke, 2019). Furthermore, I use this standard form to include descriptions of disciplinary approaches that are not always labelled with the word 'thinking' at all, because other prefixes and suffixes are also prominent, but are used with similar meanings:

- *'mindset'* is used to characterise the approaches taken in entrepreneurship and design, as in 'entrepreneurial mindset' (e.g. Daspit et al., 2023; Haynie et al., 2010), 'design mindset' (Lavrsen et al., 2023) and 'design thinking mindset' (e.g. Schweitzer et al., 2016);
- *'habits of mind'* is used to characterise the approaches taken in engineering and mathematics, as in 'engineering habits of mind' (e.g. Lucas et al., 2014) and 'mathematical habits of mind' (e.g. Cuoco et al., 1996);
- *'attitude'* is used to characterise the approaches taken in science, as in 'scientific attitude' (e.g. Gardner, 1975; Gauld & Hukins, 1980; Noll, 1935)[7];
- *'logics'* is used to characterise the approaches taken in entrepreneurship, as in 'effectuation logics' (e.g. Sarasvathy, 2021).

Just as something needn't be called '[discipline] thinking' to be included in my analysis, it is also the case that something can be named in that way and still be excluded. The main reason for such exclusions is where a reference to '[discipline] thinking' is really a reference to a stage-based process, such as with a 'design thinking process' (e.g. see Razzouk & Shute, 2012).[8] Similar distinctions could be made between systems thinking and a systems modelling process (e.g. see Meadows, 2008) or between scientific thinking and the scientific

---

[7] Although they sound similar, I do not find work on 'styles of thinking' (Crombie, 1988) and 'styles of reasoning' (Hacking, 1994) directly relevant here. This is because those terms are being used to characterise different approaches taken in the history of science, rather than (for example) the different approaches of different sciences.

[8] Note that much of the confusion or disagreement in the design thinking discourse could be resolved, or at least reduced, by specifying whether any description of, or claim made about, design thinking is directed at a design thinking mindset, at a design thinking process or at design thinking tools (other similar distinctions are discussed later). The same can be said for discourse on the other disciplinary approaches.

method (Gauld & Hukins, 1980). Such process descriptions are excluded here even though disciplinary processes could influence disciplinary approaches, and even though disciplinary approaches could involve practitioners having the inclination to adopt certain processes. I still exclude such processes from my analysis because descriptions of the stages that a practitioner follows, and the activities performed at each stage, are quite different to descriptions of the components that make up a practitioner's thinking abilities, habits of mind, attitudes, and so on. Examining the relationships between processes and approaches is no doubt interesting, but I place that outside the scope of the present work.[9]

Even having placed certain topics out of bounds, it is probably clear that the scope of this work remains rather broad. This is because it is disciplinary approaches – *in general* – that are of interest, rather than any specific disciplinary approach. With so many disciplines to consider, it is difficult to know where to start one's investigations, and also difficult to know where to start in illustrating one's findings. However, I'll begin with design thinking because that might be expected to be of most interest to readers of this series, given that design is so closely associated with creativity and imagination. Design thinking is also, conveniently, one of the most prominent disciplinary approaches (see Figure 2), and so for many readers, it will provide an accessible route into the broad landscape of other approaches.

Having considered design thinking first, I'll then move onto the other disciplinary approaches that are most easily associated with it, or are thought to complement it, such as systems thinking and entrepreneurial thinking. Next, I'll progress onto a range of other disciplinary approaches, including computational thinking, engineering thinking, statistical thinking, scientific thinking, mathematical thinking, geographical thinking, historical thinking, anthropological thinking, and so on. Where possible, I'll loosely follow that general order with the aim of providing some consistency and permitting some anticipation of how and when disciplines will be referred to. However, this ordering is not intended to imply some hierarchy of importance or relevance, and I hope that readers who have interests in disciplines that appear later in the list – *or other disciplines altogether* – are able to read this work in a way that easily connects with their concerns. My intention is to emphasise the types of things that disciplinary approaches are, and the types of relationships they have to each other, irrespective of which particular disciplines are being considered.

---

[9] What is also out of scope is how disciplinary approaches are developed and applied. That might sound strange, but I take the phenomenon of interest here to be the emergence of discussions about disciplinary approaches in numerous disconnected literatures. It would be another study entirely to understand how a person or group develop and adopt a specific disciplinary approach.

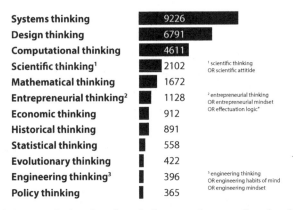

Figure 2 Bar graph showing the relative prominence of twelve forms of disciplinary approach in the scientific literature. The numbers represent the count of documents returned when searching the Scopus database for each term (title, abstract and keywords from 1954 until the search date of February 2023). Where other similar terms accounted for more than 10 per cent of the documents returned (or were determined to be significant from narrative review), these were included. In total, the literatures associated with twenty-seven disciplinary approaches were reviewed, and those returning the highest document counts are presented here. See online Appendix A for the underlying data (www.cambridge.org/Crilly).

3 Describing Disciplinary Approaches

Having made some clarifications about terminology and scope, let's turn our attention to the projects that seek to describe individual disciplinary approaches. Why are those projects undertaken? Are the resulting descriptions consistent with each other? And just what kind of thing is being described? We'll look at each of these questions in turn, before examining descriptions of individual approaches in detail.

3.1 Why Describe Disciplinary Approaches?

A common feature of many of the projects describing individual disciplinary approaches is an effort to direct attention away from the specifics of a discipline's practice and toward its intellectual or practical essence. In contrast, the disciplinary specifics – such as subject matter, tools and techniques – are described as a distraction that misleads people as to what really characterises or constitutes that discipline, especially the thinking involved. For example, Brown (2008) famously contrasted the integrative and innovative role of designers with the public's perceptions of design as a merely stylistic activity:

Historically, design has been treated as a downstream step in the development process—the point where designers, who have played no earlier role in the substantive work of innovation, come along and put a beautiful wrapper around the idea [. . . but] design thinking can lead to innovation that goes beyond aesthetics (pp. 2, 7).

What's especially interesting is that it seems many disciplines feel misunderstood in the way Brown describes. This is stated particularly clearly in discussions of geographical and historical thinking, approaches that many people might imagine they already understand from their schooling:

the public perception of geography is as a fact-based rather than conceptual discipline. This article is an attempt to challenge that *Trivial Pursuit* view of geography; it argues against the view that our discipline is just a gazetteer of place-names or a list of imports and exports, and makes a case for the power of thinking geographically. Geography, I argue, enables a unique way of seeing the world, of understanding complex problems and thinking about inter-connections at a variety of scales (from the global to the local). (P. Jackson, 2006, p. 199)

historical thinking, in its deepest forms, is neither a natural process nor something that springs automatically from psychological development. Its achievement, I argue, actually goes against the grain of how we ordinarily think. This is one of the reasons why it is much easier to learn names, dates, and stories than it is to change the fundamental mental structures that we use to grasp the meaning of the past. (Wineburg, 2010, p. 84)

Similar points have been made across a wide range of projects describing disciplinary approaches. For example, systems thinking should not be mistaken for computer modelling (Meadows, 2008, p. 6), computational thinking should not be mistaken for computer programming (Wing, 2006, p. 34) and scientific thinking should not be mistaken for scientific knowledge (Gauld & Hukins, 1980, p. 109). Clearly, in describing disciplinary approaches, many people have been concerned that their own disciplines have previously been confused for the specifics of their subject matter or their techniques, rather than the underlying essence of their practice, whatever that might be. Abstraction is seemingly the preferred way to move beyond such distracting details, revealing what lies beneath.

A consequence of abstracting from the specifics of disciplinary practices is that the resulting descriptions are no longer tied so closely to those disciplines' traditional domains of application. As such, it is a feature of many projects that they advocate for the wide-ranging applicability of the disciplinary approaches that they are describing. These are approaches that can ostensibly be learnt by many people outside the originating discipline and implemented by them in many contexts or domains. For example, in promoting design thinking, Pressman (2018) insists that it is '[n]ot just for architects or product developers, [but] can be applied across many disciplines to solve real world problems and reconcile dilemmas [, . . . in] politics and society, business, health and science, law, and writing' (pp. xvii–xviii). Similarly, but now considering systems thinking, and especially the capacity to distinguish multiple system levels, Wilensky and Resnick (1999) say that the need for this 'arises in many different domains, among many different types of learners' (p. 3). To give just one more example, Wing (2006) claims that, '[c]omputational thinking is a fundamental skill for everyone, not just for computer scientists [and therefore . . .] we should add computational thinking to every child's analytical ability' (p. 33). In response to this last proposal, Barr and Stephenson (2011) report on work that formalises the components of computational thinking, with suggestions for how those can be introduced across a range of school subjects, including maths, science, social studies and language arts. So, once abstracted from their specific application domains, and framed in general terms, many forms of disciplinary approach are celebrated for their wide-ranging applicability: if only everyone would pay attention, not get distracted by the details, and think like a practitioner of . . . [insert your favourite discipline here].

Although it is not the main focus of this present work, it is important to acknowledge that the codification and application of disciplinary approaches is seemingly successful. Representations of things like design thinking are typically driven by practical goals rather than deep conceptual commitments or theoretical agendas. The challenge is capturing enough about the disciplinary approach so that it can be understood and applied by others, often influencing their own training and practice in a relatively short period. To this end, there are, just as examples, accounts of the successful application of design thinking in business contexts (Liedtka et al., 2013), of systems thinking in healthcare development (Bashford et al., 2018) and of entrepreneurial thinking in institutional restructuring (Jacob et al., 2003). Other disciplinary approaches are often more oriented toward educational outcomes in school settings, but there too we find reports of how training in specific disciplinary approaches positively influences outcomes in the associated disciplines and sometimes also in others. For examples, see studies of the effectiveness of training in computational thinking (Scherer et al., 2019), mathematical thinking (Algani & Jmal, 2020), evolutionary thinking (Novick & Catley, 2016), geographical thinking (Karkdijk et al., 2013) and historical thinking (Keleşzade et al., 2018).

3.2 Are the Descriptions Agreed Upon?

Despite the apparent success of promoting and applying disciplinary approaches, there can be some inconsistency in the claims made about just what kind of thing they actually are. This has led to complaints, in many of the projects, that the central concepts under consideration are not well understood. For example, discussions of design thinking often engage with the problem of how poorly defined the concept is, and how the term is used in overlapping and conflicting ways. To illustrate, here are just three examples: Kimbell (2011) says that 'those who support [design thinking's] application to business or more broadly to public services or social problems, have trouble articulating what it is' (pp. 288–289); Johansson-Sköldberg et al. (2013) say that 'the design thinking discourse ... has different meanings depending on its context' (p. 121) and Patel and Mehta (2017) say that '[t]here is a lack of consensus amongst prominent champions of design thinking about its precise definition' (p. 516). The result of all this is that there are many attempts to explicitly *make sense of* design thinking, either in general, or for specific communities (e.g. see Antle, 2017; Inns & Mountain, 2020; Madson, 2021).

Although complaints about the diffuse meaning of design thinking point exclusively at that term or concept, this really isn't a problem that is unique to just one disciplinary approach. The literatures on many other approaches have also complained about the vague and inconsistent meanings of their terms. For example, in describing systems thinking, Stave and Hopper (2007) explain that 'although the goal of getting people to think more systemically is broadly shared in the system dynamics community, the term "systems thinking" is used in a variety of sometimes conflicting ways' (p. 1). Or, writing of computational thinking (CT), Shute et al. (2017) complain that 'CT definitions vary in their operationalization ... The definition of CT is evolving as researchers begin to aggregate knowledge about CT' (p. 144). Or, writing of scientific thinking, Gauld and Hukins (1980) say '[o]ne of the problems which faces a reviewer in such an area as this is the lack of agreement about the meanings to be attributed to various terms that are used' (p. 131). To give just one more example, in concluding an edited book focussed exclusively on mathematical thinking, Sternberg (1996) writes that

> In reading through the chapters of this volume, it becomes clear that there is no consensus on what mathematical thinking is, nor even on the abilities or predispositions that underlie it. If one were to start the volume with little conception of the definitions of mathematical thinking, one might end the volume with many conceptions whose relations to each other are not completely clear. (p. 303)

Seemingly, all significant projects to define and codify disciplinary approaches have encountered the same problem of vague and varying meanings of their central concepts. Each project discusses this problem as though it is a characteristic feature of the specific disciplinary approach being considered – *and an individual failing of that project* – but really it is just a feature of all such projects. Although only writing about scientific thinking, Gauld and Hukins (1980, quoted above) offer a multi-point explanation for why this imprecision prevails in that long-running project, an explanation that I here generalise to the wider set of projects trying to describe any disciplinary approach:[10]

1. few projects to define a specific disciplinary approach engage with the relevant research on more general forms of thinking, or habits of mind;
2. few projects connect with the philosophical study of the relevant discipline (e.g. philosophy of design, philosophy of science), even though different conceptions of the discipline would lead to different conceptions of that discipline's approach;
3. sometimes a specific disciplinary approach is defined as a single holistic thing, and sometimes as being made up of a set of components;
4. where components are defined, this is often done without any indication of the relationships between them; sometimes two or more components might appear to be the same as each other, or they might overlap, or one might subsume the other, or one might entail the other, and so on;
5. it is seldom acknowledged that some components might conflict with each other, for example when those components describe practitioners as being persistent yet flexible, or critical yet open-minded;
6. the lists of components that define any specific disciplinary approach have typically been developed through consultation with subject matter experts or practitioners, not psychologists, so the use of words like 'thinking', 'attitudes' or 'habits of mind' need not conform to accepted technical understandings of those words (see Gauld & Hukins, 1980, pp. 130–134).

Perhaps sitting above the six points provided by Gauld and Hukins is a more general point: projects to define different forms of disciplinary approach struggle with imprecision because those projects are very ambitious. Disciplines can be large and complex things, with considerable variation in how individuals and groups draw the boundaries around those disciplines, and also within them. The practitioners and practices that make up those disciplines are also varied, and so arriving at a simple yet comprehensive distillation of those practitioners' disciplinary approaches is unlikely to be a simple process that yields consistent

---

[10] As with the complaints in other disciplines, Gauld and Hukins (1980), say ' [o]ne of the problems which faces a reviewer in such an area as this is the lack of agreement about the meanings to be attributed to various terms that are used ... One is struck by the inadequacy, in the research literature, of the theoretical framework within which discussion about what the scientific attitude is and how it is measured takes place' (p. 129).

results. Rather than complaining, we could recognise that a multitude of definitions for each disciplinary approach is a meaningful characteristic of the projects, rather than a sign of their failure; we could embrace pluralism.[11] For example, focussing on design thinking, Carlgren et al. (2016) tell us that '[t]here is a need for a description . . . that is less normative and static and that is specific enough to be able to frame it as a concept, yet flexible enough to allow for variety in its local use' (p. 49). Looking to other disciplines, we see that Sternberg (1996) does not just observe the inconsistent definition of mathematical thinking (as quoted above), but also notes that it could be an error to try to identify any particular features that are common to all the various kinds of mathematical thinking that are discussed (p. 303). Instead, Sternberg suggests that what connects different conceptions of mathematical thinking is more a matter of 'family resemblances' (after Wittgenstein, 1968, p. 32) or 'prototypes' (after Rosch, 1973). In describing mathematical thinking – *or any other disciplinary approach* – there might be some features that are characteristic, but perhaps none of those features are necessary or definitive.

Reference to the concepts of family resemblances or prototypical class members might help us to understand the relations not just between *different descriptions of a single disciplinary approach* (such as two variants of design thinking), but also between *different disciplinary approaches* (such as a variant of design thinking and a variant of systems thinking). The outputs from a project to define a particular disciplinary approach might all bear some resemblance to each other or be related to some typical description, but there is not necessarily any feature (or component) that they all share. Similarly, the various outputs from projects to define different disciplinary approaches might also resemble each other or some prototype, but they also need not necessarily have any single common feature.[12] For example, not every variant of design thinking contains a component related to 'empathy'. More generally, not every description of a disciplinary approach needs to highlight the same perspective on that discipline, such as a practitioner's mindsets or the focus of their attention. That might cause some confusion – *and seemingly frustration* – but it is probably representative of what is happening. Those people describing disciplinary approaches are looking at subtle, complex and shifting things (i.e. the actual disciplines) and working to provide definite, simple and static descriptions of them (i.e. the specified approaches). This is always done from those people's own

---

[11] For a general discussion of theoretical pluralism, see (Griffiths, 1997).

[12] We are here just moving between different levels of abstraction in the concepts being discussed, relating variants to an individual disciplinary approach (specific-to-general), or different disciplinary approaches to the overall concept of disciplinary approaches (specific-to-general) (see Figure 1).

perspectives, even if such perspectives are often left unstated. The resulting descriptions of the disciplines are seldom offensive – *and are often very useful* – to people from outside the disciplines. However, the same descriptions can seem overly reductive to people inside the disciplines, people who adopt a more critical orientation to the representation of something they already understand well.

Despite confusion over definitions, one thing that is very consistent across the different literatures that describe specific disciplinary approaches is that they are each promoted, at least implicitly, as the good and proper way to think and act, either within that discipline or more widely. For example, Kimbell (2011) observes that 'design thinking is meant to encompass everything good about designerly practices' (p. 289). Similarly, Daspit et al. (2023) recognise that the study of entrepreneurial thinking has focussed exclusively on 'the positive aspect of the mindset', and they note that researchers have not studied any 'potentially deleterious effects' (p. 24). Perhaps this positivity is not surprising, as these projects to define disciplinary approaches typically aim to capture and codify something like the behaviour of disciplinary experts, and both the disciplines and the experts are viewed as valuable.[13] However, an alternative focus for projects looking to describe disciplinary approaches would be to capture the weaknesses or biases of each discipline, including those exhibited by its expert practitioners. For a rare example of such an analysis, see Blackwell et al.'s (2008) critique of how descriptions of computational thinking have unreflectively promoted abstraction. In contrast, these authors illustrate the negative consequences of the overapplication of abstraction in computer science, to the detriment of the products produced, the users' experiences of those products and society more generally. In a similar vein, design discourse has seen criticisms of the indiscriminate promotion of empathy (Heylighen & Dong, 2019) and ambiguity (Stacey & Eckert, 2003). Although these two criticisms don't focus on design thinking, *per se*, they address concepts that are often central to that disciplinary approach (e.g. see Micheli et al., 2019; Schweitzer et al., 2016).

3.3 What Kind of Thing Is a Disciplinary Approach?

Some of the confusion and disagreement over disciplinary approaches might stem from a lack of consistency over how disciplinary approaches are described or categorised. If we ask *what kind of thing* design thinking is (or systems thinking, etc.), it is often hard to find a complete or consistent answer in the relevant literatures. To be clear, it is not hard to find arguments that a certain

---

[13] For a criticism of this descriptive-prescriptive position, see arguments made by Vermaas (2016).

discipline's approach is important, should be widely understood, and is made up of certain components. It's that these such arguments are often made without any clear discussion of just what kind of thing is important, and so on. Is that disciplinary approach a set of skills, habits, inclinations or something else? We generally can't be sure.

Staying with design thinking as the example of central interest, it has seemingly been considered as many different kinds of thing. Reviewing the published work, Kimbell (2011) describes design thinking under three categories: 'as a cognitive style, as a general theory of design, and as a resource for organizations' (p. 285). Similarly, Hassi and Laakso (2011) describe design thinking as including 'practices, thinking styles, and mentality', each of which includes 'methods, values, and concepts' (p. 1). In a later review, Schweitzer et al. (2016) indicate that design thinking has variously been described in terms of 'design principles, thinking modes, creative behaviours and postures' (p. 72). Finally, in yet another review, Micheli et al. (2019) report that 'some authors have considered design thinking to be an organizational attribute, whereas others conceive of it at the individual level, highlighting the traits of "design thinkers"' (p. 125). So, even within the project to describe just one disciplinary approach, we can see considerable variety in the types of things that approach is taken to be or taken to include.

Looking beyond design thinking, Kaur and Craven (2020) say of systems thinking that the '[d]efinitions put forward emphasise different foci, ranging from systems thinking as a set of characteristics, systems thinking as comprised of a purpose and what it does, or systems thinking as a system itself' (p. 193).[14] Similarly, Stave and Hopper (2007) acknowledge that 'some system dynamicists see it [systems thinking] as the foundation of system dynamics as well as a number of other systems analysis approaches; others see systems thinking as a subset of system dynamics' (p. 1). Turning to entrepreneurial thinking, Daspit et al. (2023) review existing definitions of that approach and find it to be an 'ability', 'rules of thumb', 'individual beliefs', a 'perspective', personal 'qualities', 'motives, skills, and thought processes' and a form of 'thinking and decision-making' (p. 7). Clearly, it is not just design thinking that is thought to be more than one kind of thing.

Descriptions of computational thinking might at first seem simpler because Wing describes it as 'a fundamental skill' (2006, p. 33) and 'a kind of analytical thinking' (2008, p. 3717), which would straightforwardly make computational thinking an analytical thinking skill (for a review of computational thinking as way of thinking, see Selby & Woollard, 2014). However, in summarising the

---

[14] Citations have been omitted.

educational movement around computational thinking, Denning and Tedre (2021) describe that movement as having settled on the following definition: 'Designing computations that get computers to do jobs for us' (p. 30). This seemingly renders computational thinking as a design activity rather than a thinking skill, although perhaps it's the thinking skill required to undertake such an activity. Looking elsewhere, Jackson (2006) describes 'geographical thinking' as 'a unique way of seeing the world' (p. 199), and other disciplines have offered similarly varied, and often similarly brief descriptions of the kind of thing their approach is.

If we change focus, then we find that when the motivations behind descriptions of disciplinary approaches are made explicit, this tends to be very revealing about the kind of thing that is actually being described. For example, consider Andrews and Burke's (2007), reflections on what they are trying to achieve in defining historical thinking:

> If our understandings of the past constituted a sort of craft knowledge, how could we distill and communicate habits of mind we and our colleagues had developed through years of apprenticeship, guild membership, and daily practice . . . ? (unpaged)

Note the similarities with Meadows' (2008) description of her motivation for writing a book about systems thinking:

> one of the Dartmouth engineering professors watched us in seminars for a while, and then dropped by our offices. 'You people are different,' he said. 'You ask different kinds of questions. You see things I don't see. Somehow you come at the world in a different way. How? Why?' . . . That's what I hope to get across in this book. (p. 6)

So, we could perhaps add *craft knowledge* to our list of things that disciplinary approaches are. We could also add something that captures *how you come at the world*, while recognising that disciplinary approaches might be characterised by the tacit knowledge that is accumulated through training, work and social interactions.

In surveying just some of the projects that have tried to define their own disciplinary approaches, we might learn that these approaches are described as ways of thinking, habits of mind, perspectives, attitudes, cognitive styles, thinking skills, craft skills, mindsets, logics, personal traits, perspectives, and so on. However, if someone were to suggest that a particular way of thinking (or habit of mind, or perspective, etc.) should be listed as a component of a discipline's approach, what criteria should be used to assess such a claim? How do we establish what is to be included in – *and excluded from* – any particular discipline's approach? We seemingly will not find guidance on this in any of the projects we have been examining, but some hints can be found elsewhere, in fact in a completely different body of work.

In discussing the context-bound nature of cognitive skills, Perkins and Salomon (1989) offer four requirements for what they call 'general cognitive skills'. We can use these four requirements to limit what's included in disciplinary approaches, because these requirements seem to be already implicit in the various projects that discuss those approaches:

1. it must be something that practitioners actually use ('seeming use');
2. it must play an important role in their practice;
3. it must be transferrable by those practitioners to other domains;
4. it must be commonly absent from other disciplines (Perkins & Salomon, 1989, pp. 19–20).

Some projects would also – *often implicitly* – add an additional requirement:

5. it must be learnable by non-practitioners for application to their own domain.[15]

These requirements are useful to keep in mind because anyone in any discipline might exhibit a great many different ways of thinking (or habits of mind, or perspectives, etc.). However, not all of these will play an important role in their practice, or perhaps cannot be transferred to other domains (or other people), or might be commonly present in other disciplines. To give a simple example, designers might think numerically when estimating a production run or dimensioning a product, but quantitative analysis is not typically included in descriptions of design thinking because it is not *especially associated* with the discipline of design. As Dorst (2011) tells us, 'many of the activities that designers do are quite universal, and thus it would be inappropriate to claim these as exclusive to design or "Design Thinking"' (pp. 525–526). The same is true for all disciplinary approaches, because in the complex realities of any practice, many different kinds of things are done, not all of which are said to be characteristic. Rules for deciding on what gets admitted to a description of a disciplinary approach (like the five outlined above) are seldom stated, perhaps because that would

---

[15] Relevant to my goal here is that in considering two different forms of disciplinary approach, Kelly and Gero (2021) offer a clearer concept than many of those who consider only a single approach in isolation. Characterising design thinking and computational thinking, they say that 'each was inspired by a body of knowledge and expertise—design and computer science, respectively—that was recognized as valuable, and each can be understood as a transfer of a way of thinking from a particular tradition to something that is useful far more broadly' (p. 1). This clarity is probably also assisted by their comparing these disciplinary approaches to higher-order thinking skills like critical and creative thinking (discussed later).

require comparison to other disciplines, a cross-disciplinary perspective that is generally not adopted in the projects we are discussing here.

Considering all of the above, I propose the following working definition of 'disciplinary approach', one that seems to be consistent with a range of meanings already apparent – *even if implicit* – in various literatures:

> DEFINITION 1 – A disciplinary approach is a way of thinking (interpreted broadly) that influences how practitioners in a particular discipline see the world, orient toward it and act upon it. This approach is used by practitioners in ways that are important to their practice, are distinctive to their discipline, are commonly absent from other disciplines and are transferrable to other domains. This approach is also sometimes required to be learnable by those outside the discipline for application to their own domains.

Referring back to our consideration of family resemblances and prototypical class memberships, this definition needn't be read as a statement of all the characteristics that any disciplinary approach will have, but as a list of the many features that they draw from; a prototypical disciplinary approach might exhibit many or all of them. I'll revisit and expand this definition later, once we have reviewed the components that various disciplinary approaches are made up of, but for now, it will help to clarify the kind of thing these approaches are. Here and later, even though a desire for clarity and consistency imposes some restrictions on the definitions I propose, they are intended to describe current usage rather than stipulating correct meanings.

4 Collecting Disciplinary Approaches

Having characterised, in a general sense, the ambitions and confusions of the projects to describe disciplinary approaches, I now turn to considering their outputs. I do this by tabulating the components of twelve disciplinary approaches, starting with design thinking, systems thinking and entrepreneurial thinking (Tables 1–3, respectively). I then extend this to computational thinking, engineering thinking, scientific thinking, evolutionary thinking, mathematical thinking, statistical thinking, geographical thinking, historical thinking and anthropological thinking (Tables 4–12, respectively). Each table details just one variant of each approach, including the original name provided by the authors, a full list of its components, the definition of each component (where available) and anything that the components are explicitly contrasted against. There is also a summary of the main methods used to identify the components, and any associated notes of clarification. This consistent tabulation permits comparison within and across disciplines, and so interested readers will be able to investigate matters that I do not consider here.

4.1 What Is Design Thinking?

The term 'design thinking' means many different overlapping things. In scientific studies of design cognition, it is sometimes used to describe the mental processes and representations of designers (e.g. trained professionals) when they are undertaking general or specialised design tasks (for a collection of works, see Hay et al., 2020). However, this use of the term is largely (but not entirely) disconnected from more popular uses that emphasise how adopting a design-like approach can benefit a wide range of practices, professions and sectors (for a recent commentary on the distinction, see Cross, 2023). This more popular interpretation of design thinking is sometimes considered controversial for not representing the practices of expert designers or for not acknowledging the skills required to apply design processes (for an example critique, see Kolko, 2018). Nevertheless, the popular use of the term prevails, typically emphasising empathy, visualisation, iteration and creativity. For example, these components can be seen in the variant of design thinking summarised in Table 1, which is itself derived from other variants.

4.2 What Is Systems Thinking?

Just as with 'design thinking', the term 'systems thinking' means many different overlapping things. In some instances, it describes a form of thinking that is taken to be central to disciplines like ecology (Stiling, 1994), or to systems-focussed sub-disciplines, such as systems engineering and systems biology (Camelia & Ferris, 2016; Momsen et al., 2022). In other instances, it is taken to be the kind of thinking that is exhibited by (or required by) those who construct specific systems representations, such as models of systems dynamics (Richmond, 1993, 2016). However, 'systems thinking' is perhaps most commonly interpreted as a generally applicable thinking skill, or set of skills, that can be applied across many practices, professions and sectors (e.g. M. C. Jackson, 2003). These descriptions of systems thinking typically emphasise a focus on holism, relationships and interactions, as compared to analytic reductionism. The variant summarised in Table 2, emphasises the biological and ecological origins of some systems perspectives.

4.3 What Is Entrepreneurial Thinking?

Just as with 'design thinking' and 'systems thinking', the term 'entrepreneurial thinking' also means many different overlapping things. In some instances, there is a focus on the cognitive aspects of entrepreneurial behaviour (Grégoire et al., 2011), while in others there is a focus on something more like the inclinations or 'logics' employed by entrepreneurs (Sarasvathy, 2001). Descriptions of

Table 1 Micheli et al.'s description of design thinking.

Published work: (Micheli et al., 2019)
Approach label: 'Design thinking'
Main methods: Systematic review and card sorting
Note: These ten 'principal attributes of design thinking' are distinguished from eight other methods that support them.

Component labels	Component definitions	Contrast
'Creativity and innovation'	The production and implementation of novel and useful ideas.	–
'User-centeredness and involvement'	Gaining empathy for diverse groups, either through research or participatory processes to address both expressed and latent needs.	–
'Problem solving'	Addressing 'wicked' or 'ill-structured' problems with confusing or incomplete information and with conflicting values.	–
'Iteration and experimentation'	Trial-and-error learning based on testing a range of possible solutions as sketches and prototypes (often with users). This triggers problem definition and experimental solution creation.	–
'Interdisciplinary collaboration'	Bringing people together from different departments, units, organizations and functions to address project complexity, and ensure that technical, business and human dimensions of a problem are all represented.	–
'Ability to visualize'	Moving from abstract thinking to visualizing ideas and then using those visualizations to guide an emerging rather than deterministic inquiry.	–
'Gestalt view'	Adopting an integrative approach that enables both the development of a deeper understanding of the problem context and the identification of relevant insights.	–

'Abductive reasoning'	The imagination of what might be (rather than the analysis of what is). Adopting an attitude toward workable solutions that is assertion-based rather than evidence-based.
'Tolerance of ambiguity and failure'	Accepting 'equivocal information and failure'. Able to 'embrace ambiguity and engage in iterative cycles of trial-and-error experiments and stakeholder feedback'.
'Blending analysis and intuition'	Combining a focus on research and evidence with 'felt knowledge about patterns and holistic associations'. Jointly emphasising 'exploration and exploitation, reliability and validity, and declarative and modal logic'.

Table 2 Capra & Luisi's description of systems thinking.

Published work: (Capra & Luisi, 2014, pp. 80–82)
Approach label: 'Systems thinking' (as contrasted with 'Analytical thinking')
Main method: Literature review (interdisciplinary)
Note: '[A]ll these shifts of perspective are really just different ways of saying the same thing. Systems thinking means a shift of perception from material objects and structures to the nonmaterial processes and patterns of organization that represent the very essence of life'.

Component labels	Component definitions	Contrast
'From the parts to the whole'	'Living systems are integrated wholes whose properties cannot be reduced to those of smaller parts. Their essential, or 'systemic', properties are properties of the whole, which none of the parts have. They arise from patterns of organization that are characteristic of a particular class of systems. Systemic properties are destroyed when a system is dissected, either physically or conceptually, into isolated elements'.	–
'Inherent multidisciplinarity'	'The systems view of life teaches us that all living systems share a set of common properties and principles of organization. This means that systems thinking is inherently multidisciplinary. It can be applied to integrate academic disciplines and to discover similarities between different phenomena within the broad range of living systems'.	–
'From objects to relationships'	'At each level the living system is an integrated whole with smaller components, while at the same time being a part of a larger whole. … . Therefore, the shift of perspective from the parts to the whole can also be seen as a shift from objects to relationships'.	–

'From measuring to mapping'	'In science, we have been told, things need to be measured and weighed. But relationships cannot be measured and weighed; relationships need to be mapped. . . . Networks, cycles, and boundaries are examples of patterns of organization that are characteristic of living systems and are at the center of attention in systems science'.
'From quantities to qualities'	Mapping relationships and studying patterns is not a quantitative but a qualitative approach. Thus, systems thinking implies a shift from quantities to qualities.
'From structures to processes'	In systems science, every structure is seen as the manifestation of underlying processes. Systems thinking includes a shift of perspective from structures to processes.
'From objective to epistemic science'	'In Cartesian science, scientific descriptions were believed to be objective – that is, independent of the human observer and the process of knowing. Systems science, by contrast, implies that epistemology – the understanding of the process of knowing – has to be included explicitly in the description of natural phenomena'.
'From Cartesian certainty to approximate knowledge'	'In the systemic paradigm it is recognized that all scientific concepts and theories are limited and approximate. Science can never provide any complete and definitive understanding. In science, to put it bluntly, we never deal with truth, in the sense of a precise correspondence between our descriptions and the described phenomena. We always deal with limited and approximate knowledge'.

entrepreneurial thinking typically emphasise many components that overlap with design thinking, including an orientation toward customers and iterative problem solving based on experimentation (Frederiksen & Brem, 2017). In contrast, the variant of entrepreneurial thinking summarised in Table 3 focusses on five key 'principles' that entrepreneurs employ.

4.4 What Is Computational Thinking?

Just like the three disciplinary approaches already discussed, and those that are discussed in the following sections, the term 'computational thinking' means many different and overlapping things. (Terms like these are debated and contested in similar ways across disciplines, and so I won't now emphasise that further.) Common to many descriptions of computational thinking is a focus on the modes of thought that computer scientists exhibit, in comparison to the skills required when using computers (e.g. Wing, 2006). Computational thinking is sometimes distinguished from writing computer code, with emphasis instead placed on how more general 'practices' like abstraction,

Table 3 Sarasvathy's description of entrepreneurial thinking

Published work: (Sarasvathy, 2009, pp. 74–95)
Approach label: 'Effectuation logic' (in contrast to 'Causal reasoning')
Main method: Observation study

Component labels	Component definitions	Contrast
'The bird in the hand principle'	Start with the resources available to you (who you are, what you know and who you know), rather than what you want to achieve.	–
'The affordable loss principle'	Focus on what you can afford to lose in pursuing an opportunity, rather than what you stand to gain.	–
'The lemonade principle'	Translate changing circumstances into opportunities (through action), rather than viewing them as setbacks.	–
'The crazy quilt principle'	Enrol others into your venture on the basis of the resources they have and what they can afford to lose.	–
'The pilot in the plan principle'	Work so as to shape the future, rather than trying to predict it.	–

incrementalism, iteration and reuse can be applied in non-computational contexts (Barr & Stephenson, 2011). These components can be seen in the variant of computational thinking summarised in Table 4, which is itself derived from other variants.

Table 4 Kong's description of computational thinking.

Published work: (Kong, 2019)
Approach label: 'Computational thinking practices'
Main method: Literature review
Note: 'The challenge of introducing Computation Thinking (CT) education to K−12 is how to evaluate learners' CT development. This study used information from previous studies to identify essential components and methods for evaluation'. These practices are distinguished from computational thinking concepts: loops; conditionals; sequences; parallelism; data structures (such as variables and lists); mathematical operators, functions and Boolean operators; event handling; procedures; initialisation.

Component labels	Component definitions	Contrast
'Abstraction', 'modelling' and 'modularising'	[Abstraction is not defined] Modelling requires people to 'organize data, structure their thoughts, describe relationships, and analyse proposed designs'; Modularising requires people to 'build something large by putting together collections of smaller parts'.	−
'Algorithmic thinking'	'Define the steps and develop instructions to solve a problem'.	−
'Testing and debugging'	'[S]everal attempts must be made before all errors are eliminated'.	−
'Being iterative and incremental'	'[D]evelop a little bit, then try it out, then develop more'.	−
'Problem decomposition'	'[B]reaking down problems into smaller, more manageable tasks'.	−
'Planning and designing'	Plan solutions before coding during programming.	Trial-and -error
'Reusing and remixing'	'[P]roduce more complicated creations by building on existing projects or ideas'.	−

4.5 What Is Engineering Thinking?

Engineering thinking is normally distinguished from engineering domain knowledge. Different engineering disciplines draw from specific bodies of scientific knowledge, such as mechanics, structures, electronics and materials. In contrast, descriptions of engineering thinking emphasise how engineers approach the problems they are addressing and the solutions they are developing (Lucas et al., 2014). Alternatively, because engineers draw on scientific knowledge derived from disciplines such as physics and chemistry, engineering thinking is sometimes distinguished from the scientific thinking that produced such knowledge. In these instances, the focus is often placed on the engineer's drive to change situations rather than just understand them. This perspective is emphasised in the variant summarised in Table 5, which has some similarities with design thinking and entrepreneurial thinking, and includes systems thinking.

4.6 What Is Scientific Thinking?

Like engineering thinking, scientific thinking is often described in contrast to (scientific) domain knowledge, and like design thinking it is often described in contrast to the specific methods applied (here, the scientific method). Rather than emphasising knowledge and method, descriptions of scientific thinking instead emphasise the 'attitude' of scientists or their 'habits of mind'. Decades of work have been done on this, often focussing on how scientists are inclined toward accurate and critical thinking, valuing evidence over argumentation (see reviews in Dunbar & Fugelsang, 2005; Gorman, 2006). The variant of scientific thinking summarised in Table 6 is noteworthy for being formalised so much earlier than many of the other disciplinary approaches reported here.

4.7 What Is Evolutionary Thinking?

Evolutionary thinking describes the ways of thinking that are useful for understanding processes of biological evolution, including variation, selection and inheritance (Stearns, 2006; Suzuki, 2021). However, the widespread application of evolutionary thinking to non-biological entities means that this disciplinary approach can be seen in some accounts of how technologies, societies, ideas and organisations change over time (e.g. Breslin, 2016). One of the features of evolutionary thinking is flexibility in considering similarities between the members of a group, considering the variation between those members, and considering previous generations from which those members descended. This is illustrated in the variant summarised in Table 7.

Table 5 Waks et al.'s description of engineering thinking.

Published work: (Waks et al., 2011)
Approach label: 'Engineering thinking' in engineering design (in contrast to
   'Scientific research')
Main methods: Interviews and literature review
Note: 'This paper presents a characterization of engineering thinking in general,
and electric and electronic engineering thinking, in particular, from the point of
view of experienced engineers. In addition, to highlight the uniqueness of
engineering thinking, we compare engineering thinking in engineering design
and research thinking in scientific research in the area of the exact sciences'. In
addition to these six components of 'thinking', there are also components of
'Aims', 'Knowledge and tools', 'Environment' and 'Motivation for success'.

Component labels	Component definitions	Contrast
'Synthesis, aspiration to understand how'	'Build and assemble the elements of the new system in order to meet the product's requirements . . . reorganizing elements into a new pattern or structure through generating, planning, or producing'.	Analysis, aspiration to understand why
'Concrete thinking mainly'	Considerer 'human needs as perceived by human senses, and formulate them in more concrete terms than science . . . predict undesirable effects and find how to neutralize them if they appear'.	Abstract thinking mainly
'Systems thinking'	'[L]ook at the whole, and the parts, and the connections between the parts, studying the whole in order to understand the parts'.	Thinking focused on a theme
'Advance toward the desirable'	Use 'means-end analysis' to define the desirable features of the product and plan appropriate actions to realise them.	Advance toward the unknown
'Optimal solution'	'[S]trive to optimize the solution' in terms of 'effectiveness, minimal development time,	Global solution

Table 5 (cont.)

	development simplicity, cost, redundancy and their combinations'.	
'Creative thinking and algorithmic routine thinking'	Employ 'creative or 'lateral' thinking' in the very first stages of the development process to develop new ideas. Then employ a 'sequential process in which every step has to be correct and justified before moving to subsequent stage' (collectively this is 'integrative thinking').	–

4.8 What Is Mathematical Thinking?

As with scientific thinking, the long history and high status of mathematical practice have led scholars and researchers to devote considerable attention to mathematical thinking (for a collection of views, see Sternberg & Ben-Zeev, 1996). Descriptions of mathematical thinking often emphasise aspects of thought that are independent of specific mathematical operations (e.g. addition, multiplication) and also independent of what those operations are applied to (e.g. numbers, algebraic variables). Instead, the focus is on more abstract mental activities that are characteristic of mathematical work, especially the more creative aspects of that work, such as making conjectures and drawing inferences. This perspective on mathematical thinking is emphasised in the variant summarised in Table 8.

4.9 What Is Statistical Thinking?

Statistical thinking might be considered as a sub-type of mathematical thinking, focussed on a subset of operations and a subset of applications. As with mathematical thinking, the focus is typically not on specific knowledge or techniques, but on the more general way in which statisticians learn about the problem, recognise opportunities for variation and quantify that variation with data (Chance, 2002). Different dimensions of statistical thinking can be identified that are widespread in other disciplinary approaches, including problem-solving processes, general modes of thought and dispositions such as

Table 6 Noll's description of scientific thinking.

Published work: (Noll, 1935)
Approach label: 'Scientific attitude', comprising specific scientific 'habits of thinking'
Main method: Reflection on personal experience
Note: 'The titles [of the habits] as listed are probably sufficiently clear to make unnecessary any detailed description of each habit. They may, however, be briefly defined for further clarity in terms of their opposites. (p. 148)'

Component labels	Component definitions	Contrast
'Habit of accuracy in all operations, including accuracy in calculation, observation and report'	–	'[H]abits of careless, inaccurate work'.
'Habit of intellectual honesty'	–	'[H]abits as exaggeration and rationalization'.
'Habit of openmindedness'	–	Bigotry, prejudice, and intolerance.
'Habit of suspended judgment'	–	'[T]he habit of making snap judgments, or of jumping to conclusions'.
'Habit of looking for true cause and effect relationships'	–	'[H]abits of superstitious thinking, of expecting rewards to come without commensurate effort'.
'Habit of criticalness, including that of self-criticism'	–	'[H]abits of accepting explanations of phenomena without question, or without attempt at evaluation'.

scepticism, imagination, curiosity and perseverance (Wild & Pfannkuch, 1999). Some types of thinking that are more specific to statistics are summarised in the variant presented in Table 9.

4.10 What Is Geographical Thinking?

The term 'geographical thinking' is used to describe the perspectives and approaches that expert geographers exhibit and that geography educators want to encourage in their students. As with the other disciplinary approaches

Creativity and Imagination

Table 7 O'Hara's description of evolutionary thinking.

Published work: (O'Hara, 1997)
Approach label: 'Systematics' (Evolutionary thinking)
Main method: Literature review
Note: Typological thinking is referred to here as 'typology', but the term 'typological thinking' is used in the same sense elsewhere. Typological thinking is sometimes considered pre-Darwinian and is offered as a contrast with population and tree thinking (but see Lewens, 2009).

Component labels	Component definitions	Contrast
'Typological thinking'	An essentialist view that holds an instance to be an example of a type (variation is error).	–
'Population thinking'	A view that individual instances are members of a population that exhibits variation.	–
'Tree thinking'	A view that individual instances are descended from ancestors, and inherit their traits.	–

Table 8 Burton's description of mathematical thinking.

Published work: (Burton, 1984)
Approach label: 'Mathematical thinking'
Main method: Reflection on personal experience
Note: 'The following axiom underpins the approach: Thinking is the means used by humans to improve their understanding of, and exert some control over, their environment'.

Component labels	Component definitions	Contrast
'Specializing'	Examining particular examples to explore a more general a question or problem (promoting induction).	–
'Conjecturing'	Exploring, expressing, and then substantiating the relationships and underlying patterns that connect different particular examples.	–
'Generalizing'	Creating order and meaning by advancing general claims about patterns and regularity.	–
'Convincing'	Testing generalizations until they are convincing (both for the thinker and the wider world).	–

Table 9 Wild and Pfannkuch's description of statistical thinking.

Published work: (Wild & Pfannkuch, 1999)
Approach label: 'Statistical thinking'
Main methods: Student and expert interviews
Note: These 'types of thinking' are described as fundamental to statistical thinking. Other types are described as 'general', including 'strategic thinking', 'seeking explanations', 'modelling' and 'applying techniques'.

Component labels	Component definitions	Contrast
'Recognition of the need for data'	'The recognition of the inadequacies of personal experiences and anecdotal evidence leading to a desire to base decisions on deliberately collected data'.	–
'Transnumeration'	'[F]orming and changing data representations of aspects of a system to arrive at a better understanding'.	–
'Consideration of variation'	The recognition of 'omnipresent variation', requiring 'learning and decision making under uncertainty … the purposes of explanation, prediction, or control'.	–
'Reasoning with statistical models'	Model-based or framework-based thinking, where the models and frameworks are unique to the statistical approach.	–
'Integrating the statistical and contextual'	'The raw materials on which statistical thinking works are statistical knowledge, context knowledge and the information in data. The thinking itself is the synthesis of these elements to produce implications, insights and conjectures'.	–

described here, there are debates over which definitions to use, which components to include and whether or not there is value in the overall concept (for a collection of views, see Brooks et al., 2017). Again, the focus is not typically on geographers' domain knowledge (e.g. national import data) or practices (e.g. cartography), but on the more abstract and generally applicable matters that they devote their attention to, such as analysis at different levels of abstraction, and the relationships between

Table 10 Jackson's description of geographical thinking.

Published work: (P. Jackson, 2006)	

Approach label: 'Thinking geographically'
Main methods: Reflection on personal experience
Note: Motivated by the objective of focusing people's attention on the conceptual nature of the discipline. 'Relational thinking' is described as being of a 'different order' to the preceding three pairs of concepts.

Component labels	Component definitions	Contrast
'Space and place'	Distinguishing and relating concepts of physically defined spaces and socially meaningful places.	–
'Scale and connection'	Engaging with a hierarchy of scales from the body to the global, and relating them to each other (e.g. in terms of causation).	–
'Proximity and distance'	Considering physical, social and imagined distances, and how these can and cannot be bridged.	–
'Relational thinking'	Focussing on the similarities and differences of the geographies of 'us and them, self and other'.	–

things at those different levels. This can sound like a form of systems thinking, as exemplified by the variant summarised in Table 10.

4.11 What Is Historical Thinking?

The term 'historical thinking' is generally used to describe how historians think and what they think about, in contrast to the sequences of events that are sometimes taken to be matters of historical record. For example, some accounts of historical thinking state that when seeking to understand people in the past, historians are required to navigate the tension between the ways in which those people are familiar to us due to our common humanity and yet strange due to differing contexts and values (Wineburg, 2010). There is a clear connection here to accounts of anthropological thinking (see next section), and thus design thinking. Other accounts of historical thinking focus on more general concepts, such as significance, evidence, continuity, change, cause and consequence (Seixas, 2017). This links historical thinking to systems thinking, which is especially evident in the variant summarised in Table 11.

Table 11 Andrews & Burke's description of historical thinking.

Published work: (Andrews & Burke, 2007)
Approach label: 'Historical thinking'
Main method: Reflection on personal experience
Note: Motivated by the question of 'how could we distill and communicate habits of mind we and our colleagues had developed through years of apprenticeship, guild membership, and daily practice'.

Component labels	Component definitions	Contrast
'Change over time'	Attending to the things that stay the same and the things that change.	–
'Context'	Focussing on telling stories through establishing the relevant context.	–
'Causality'	The use of argumentation and evidence (rather than experimentation) to construct accounts of causal relations.	Scientific (experimental) methods of establishing causality
'Contingency'	Acknowledging the interconnectedness of outcomes, which are dependent on many prior conditions.	–
'Complexity'	Analytical rigour in making sense of moral, epistemological and causal complexity.	–

4.12 What Is Anthropological Thinking?

The term 'anthropological thinking' (and similar terms) refers to the general approaches that anthropologists take to the world. These can be conceptual approaches, such as attending to culture, values, identity and authority (Engelke, 2019), or methodological approaches, such as comparison (Binah-Pollak et al., 2024). Interestingly, Binah-Pollak et al., emphasise the adoption of a holistic perspective when considering cultural context, so that the entire system of relevance is attended to, linking to systems thinking. Much of anthropological thinking is focused on understanding groups of people and the contexts they operate in. As such it can be seen as an elaboration of the empathy component

Table 12 Tett's description of anthropological thinking.

Published work: (Tett, 2021, pp. xiv–xv)
Approach label: 'Anthrovision' (Anthropological thinking)
Main method: Reflection on personal experience
Note: Described as 'three core principles of the anthropology mindset'.

Component labels	Component definitions	Contrast
'Empathy and diversity'	Recognise what seems strange in unfamiliar settings and work to understand why things are the way they are.	–
'Self-insight'	Recognise what you learn about yourself through working to understand others.	–
'Blind spots'	Focus on what people (and you) aren't talking about and don't understand.	–

often emphasised in descriptions of design thinking. For example, empathy makes up the first component of anthropological thinking in the variant summarised in Table 12, with the other two components developing that further.

4.13 What about Other Approaches and Other Variants?

The twelve disciplinary approaches tabulated above are clearly just a subset of those that have been described in the various relevant literatures. This limitation is partly imposed by space constraints, but I have also restricted the tables to those approaches for which I found neatly delineated sets of components. I have omitted other approaches that have been described but seemingly not decomposed in this way, even if I discuss them in other sections.[16] These approaches include artistic thinking (e.g. Sullivan, 2001), craft thinking (e.g. Groth, 2016; Ings, 2015), technological thinking (e.g. Gorman, 2006), architectural thinking (e.g. Frascari, 2009), systems-architectural thinking (e.g. Aier et al., 2015), economic thinking (e.g. Heyne et al., 2013) and data-scientific thinking (e.g. Cao, 2018; Gould, 2021). Even for those approaches that *are* tabulated in this section, only one example variant is offered for each. For some or all of these approaches, there are other variants available in the literature, which can be tabulated in a similar way. Again, due to space constraints, these cannot all be summarised here for comparison, but online Appendix C (available at www.cambridge.org/Crilly) does tabulate other

---

[16] This is why the twelve approaches tabulated here are not identical to the twelve illustrated in Figure 2.

variants of design, systems, entrepreneurial and computational thinking (to illustrate differences between variants, and to support interpretation of a later figure).

5 Reviewing Components of Disciplinary Approaches

In earlier sections, we looked at variations in the kinds of things that disciplinary approaches are claimed to be, and also disagreements over the resulting descriptions of those approaches. Although the overall definitions of individual disciplinary approaches can vary greatly, these definitions are often accompanied by a description of the components that make up those approaches, as illustrated in Tables 1–12. If we want to better understand what these approaches really are and how they are related to each other then it is instructive to examine these components because they are the smaller parts from which each disciplinary whole is made up. This is especially important because sometimes the kinds of things that the parts seemingly are, are not consistent with each other, or are not consistent with the kinds of things that the wholes are claimed to be.

5.1 Are They Really about Thinking?

At the most general level, the various projects to define the disciplinary approaches are referred to in terms of 'thinking', such as 'design *thinking*', '*thinking* geographically' and '*thinking* like an economist'. It is certainly true that many of the components that each disciplinary approach is divided into appear to describe something to do with thinking. Taking design thinking as an example, one of the components that is often proposed is a specific mode of logical reasoning called 'abduction' (e.g. Dorst, 2011; Kimbell, 2011, p. 297; Micheli et al., 2019, p. 132). This can be distinguished from other modes of reasoning that are emphasised in other disciplinary approaches, such as deduction and induction in the natural sciences (e.g. Dunbar & Fugelsang, 2005, p. 712) and related components in mathematical thinking (Burton, 1984, p. 38). However, while these modes of logical reasoning might be considered as *ways of thinking*, other components might be more accurately regarded as *objects of thought*. For example, in whatever way people are thinking, they might think *about* 'non-linearity' (listed in Arnold and Wade's (2015) description of systems thinking) or *about* 'scale and connection' (listed in Jackson's (2006) description of geographical thinking).

Although various components of various disciplinary approaches are related to modes or objects of thought, this is just a subset of the types of components that are described. Examining each approach in detail reveals considerable variation in what the components describe, and this variation is visible not just between disciplinary approaches, but also within them, and within individual variants. For example, some components are seemingly a reference to

- *modes of thought*, such as those described above, but also 'abstraction' (listed in Barr and Stephenson's (2011) description of computational thinking);
- *objects of thought*, such as those described above, but also 'contingency' (listed in Andrews and Burke's (2007) description of historical thinking);
- *objects of attention*, such as the 'blind spots' that others overlook (listed in Tett's (2021) description of anthropological thinking);
- *capacities or abilities*, such as 'empathy' (listed in Schweitzer et al.'s (2016) description of design thinking);
- *actions that are taken,* such as 'the crazy quilt principle' of collaboration (listed in Sarasvathy's (2009) description of entrepreneurial thinking);
- *processes* that are followed, such as 'iteration and experimentation' (listed in Micheli et al.'s (2019) description of design thinking);
- *artefacts* that are constructed, such as visualisations and models, but also 'the minimum viable product' (listed in Frederiksen and Brem's (2017) description of entrepreneurial thinking)
- *things that are accepted, tolerated or embraced*, such as 'ambiguity and failure' (listed in Micheli et al.'s (2019) description of design thinking).

Given the various types of components that make up disciplinary approaches, one interpretation is that these approaches aren't necessarily about thinking after all. Perhaps projects describing disciplinary approaches have just used the word 'thinking' loosely, to indicate that we are now focussing more on how practitioners generally go about their work rather than the specific subject matter that they work with or the tools they use. Perhaps descriptions of disciplinary approaches are intended to include not just attitudes and inclinations, but also things like physical actions, processes and outputs. This inclusive meaning of thinking might fit better with the comparatively neutral term I have been using throughout: 'disciplinary *approach*'. Disciplinary approaches, on this account, needn't describe ways of thinking, as such, but could still describe aspects of practice that are at once characteristic of a particular discipline, while also being abstracted or generalised so that they can be understood as more widely applicable beyond that discipline.

Another interpretation is that these projects to define disciplinary approaches are indeed focussed on thinking, but that the various components they list have not always been clearly described that way. For example, perhaps those components that are seemingly describing actions, processes and outputs, should in fact be read as descriptions of the way practitioners in the relevant disciplines *think about* those things. For example, designers and engineers are known for constructing and testing provisional representations through 'prototyping' (e.g. Lucas et al., 2014; Micheli et al., 2019; Schweitzer et al., 2016), which is seemingly an action or activity involving an artefact. However, what if referring to prototyping as a component of a disciplinary approach might really mean something a bit different? What if it means the *inclination* to prototype, the *motivation* to do so, the *value* assigned to the resulting learnings, the *willingness* to respond to those learnings, the *habit* of engaging in it repeatedly and the overall *attitude* taken toward it? By framing 'prototyping' in this way it becomes more like a way of thinking than an activity. We might apply the same broad interpretation to other components that are seemingly framed as actions, processes or representations, but could instead be reframed to seem more like thinking.

5.2 Can Taxonomies of Thinking Help?

Given the common use of the term 'thinking' in describing disciplinary approaches and their components, it is perhaps surprising that general taxonomies of thinking have seemingly not been widely consulted. For example, the Cattell–Horn–Carroll theory of cognitive abilities provides structured representations of the varieties of human intelligence and achievement. The current and expanded version has six high-level categories, including 'memory and efficiency', 'acquired knowledge' and 'reasoning', and over eighty low-level items, including 'induction', 'general sequential reasoning' and 'ideational fluency' (Flanagan & Dixon, 2014). Many other such classifications of cognitive abilities can be identified (for a collection, see Newton, 2005), and there are related models showing how such abilities are connected to learning (e.g. Shute, 1994).

Focussing less on abilities, is Costa and Kallick's (2008) set of sixteen 'habits of mind', a list of attributes that characterise the approaches taken by people from all disciplines, including their many skills, attitudes, experiences and inclinations. This list was derived from studies of what successful people do 'when they are confronted with problems to solve, decisions to make, creative ideas to generate, and ambiguities to clarify' (p. 1). On the face of it, this is exactly what the projects to define disciplinary approaches are trying to identify and include. In fact, Costa and Kallick's (2008) sixteen habits of mind include some that can be mapped directly to particular components of the disciplinary approaches we have been considering so far, including

- 'listening with understanding and empathy' (e.g. see design thinking's characteristic of being 'empathetic', as reported by Schweitzer et al., 2016);
- 'taking responsible risks' (e.g. see entrepreneurial thinking's principle of 'affordable loss', as reported by Sarasvathy, 2009);
- 'striving for accuracy' (e.g. see scientific thinking's 'habit of accuracy', as reported by Noll, 1935).

Taxonomies that provide a structured understanding of thinking, learning and habits of mind are clearly relevant to how we might consider disciplinary approaches. As such, perhaps we might expect that the projects to define those approaches would start with the identification or development of a discipline-neutral taxonomy that could be drawn on for this purpose. However, such taxonomies are seldom mentioned. Instead, when individual projects develop descriptions of disciplinary approaches that are divided into components, these components are seemingly developed in an *ad hoc* fashion. They are generally not drawn from existing lists or hierarchies (for an exception, see Lucas et al.'s (2014) description of engineering thinking, which is connected to Claxton's notion of 'learning power' (Gornall et al., 2005, p. 6)).

As we saw earlier, the various projects that have focussed on defining disciplinary approaches have typically not been particularly precise in defining what kinds of things their approaches are (i.e. whether they are a way of thinking or something else). It is now apparent that those projects also haven't been very precise about what kinds of things the components of their approaches are either. To put it another way, more effort has seemingly gone into identifying and naming the various components that make up each discipline's approach than has gone into establishing what kinds of things those components are, and how those relate to the kind of thing that the disciplinary approach is. However, I'll here lean toward 'thinking' being the emphasis that is sought in these projects, rather than something more activity-oriented, such as doing or making. This is consistent with the titles these projects have generally given themselves (design thinking, etc.), and the way the projects are introduced (understanding how designers think, etc.). As such, I'll expand my earlier working definition with this in mind, now focussing on the components from which the approaches are made up, with revised content italicised:

> DEFINITION 2 – A disciplinary approach is a way of thinking (interpreted broadly) that influences how practitioners in a particular discipline see the world, orient toward it and act upon it. *Such approaches are often described as a set of components, which can be identified as ways of thinking, objects of thought, thinking skills, cognitive styles, habits of mind, mindsets, craft knowledge, attitudes, logics, perspectives, inclinations, dispositions, personal traits, values and perspectives (as distinct from subject matter knowledge, processes, actions, techniques, tools and outputs). These components are limited to those that are* used by practitioners in ways that are important to their practice, are distinctive to their discipline, are commonly absent from other disciplines and are transferrable to other domains. *The overall approach and its components* are also sometimes required to be learnable by those outside the discipline for application to their own domains.

From now on, I'll use this definition, without implying that it captures all the meanings out there, or even that all those meanings can be captured by a single definition.

6 Examining Claims about Disciplinary Approaches

Having now drawn the disciplinary approaches together and examined them closely, I will focus on how they are related to each other. For example, if designers must understand, intervene in and develop systems, then what are the connections between design thinking and systems thinking? Or, if design thinking can be applied to business contexts, and if entrepreneurs design businesses, then what overlaps might we find between design thinking and entrepreneurial thinking?[17] What connections might each of these approaches have to each other, and also to still other approaches, such as computational thinking? Questions like these can be framed in much more general terms and thus asked of all the disciplinary approaches that we have been considering. Such questions might lead us to further examine whether the disciplinary approaches are defined in relative or absolute terms, whether they are really discipline-specific or discipline-neutral, and whether sub-disciplines and inter-disciplines have been adequately accounted for.

6.1 What Are Disciplinary Approaches Defined Relative to?

One thing that we might wonder about when considering different disciplinary approaches, is what each particular approach is being contrasted with. For example, are the characteristics of design thinking somehow distinctive in themselves? Or, is it that they are distinctive in comparison to the approaches taken in some alternative disciplines such as science or art? Or is it that they are distinctive in comparison to some 'normal' or 'conventional' way of approaching things? The same questions could be asked across the range of disciplines that have undertaken projects to define their specific – *yet generalisable* – approaches. However, perhaps because each discipline has undertaken its own project in isolation from the others, there are only a few cases where the components of a disciplinary approach are defined in contrast to anything else. Here are two examples though: Richmond's (2016) definition of the components of systems thinking are compared with their opposites, which are associated with 'traditional business thinking', and Grimes and Vogus' (2021) definition of the components of entrepreneurial thinking are compared with

---

[17] For example, note that Peschl et al.'s (2021) description of entrepreneurial thinking is very similar to Micheli et al.'s (2019) description of design thinking, with many of the components being defined in near-identical ways.

alternatives from 'conventional thinking'. Perhaps a more definite and elaborated contrast is drawn by Waks et al. (2011) in their description of engineering thinking in comparison to the thinking required in 'scientific research' (see Table 5).

Pairings such as those described above do a lot to clarify what is meant by each component of a disciplinary approach because those components are then defined relative to some explicitly specified alternative. However, these pairings also generally take the form of making contrasts between the comparatively well-defined components under consideration and alternatives that are only loosely defined. What I mean by this is that while authors interested in their own disciplinary approach will cite other work on that approach and describe the components from which it is made up, any reference they make to some other discipline's approach will typically not draw from any relevant literature, and might assume it has not been decomposed. It's as though these authors are implicitly saying that '*our* disciplinary approach is complex, nuanced and debated, whereas *theirs* is simple, well understood and agreed upon' (for an example of this being recognised, see Coelen & Smulders, 2023, p. 403).

Although *the individual components* of one disciplinary approach are seldom actually defined in relation to (or in contrast to) the components of another established disciplinary approach, the *overall approaches* are sometimes compared. Given the rarity of such comparisons, spread across numerous literatures, it is valuable to explicitly acknowledge those that exist. For example, there are well-founded comparisons between design thinking and several other disciplinary approaches, including systems thinking (e.g. Buchanan, 2019; Litster et al., 2023; Pourdehnad et al., 2011), entrepreneurial thinking (e.g. Christensen et al., 2023; Garbuio et al., 2018; Klenner et al., 2022; Varadarajan, 2019) and computational thinking (e.g. Denning, 2013; Kelly & Gero, 2021). Going beyond such pair-wise comparisons, Patel and Mehta (2017) consider frameworks of design thinking, systems thinking and entrepreneurial thinking through a detailed review of the three relevant literatures and case studies of their integrated application in practice. Very unusually, Lewrick et al. (2018) actually describe such integration as characteristic of a design thinking mindset, saying that '[a]s the situation requires, we combine different approaches with design thinking, data analytics, systems thinking, and [entrepreneurial thinking]' (p. 9; also see §3.1 and §3.3).

That's all focussed on design thinking, but if we consider other disciplinary approaches, then there are similarly well-founded comparisons between computational thinking and mathematical thinking (e.g. Rycroft-Smith & Connolly, 2019; Sneider et al., 2014), and between computational thinking and systems thinking (Easterbrook, 2014; Shin et al., 2022). Again, going beyond pair-wise comparisons, Lucas et al. (2014) discuss engineering habits of mind in contrast to those found in mathematics and science (with reference to similar projects in those disciplines). Similarly, Gould (2021) describes data-scientific thinking as including decreasing proportions of statistical thinking, computational thinking and mathematical thinking. Even more wide-ranging is Shute et al.'s (2017) discussion of computational thinking in comparison to mathematical thinking, engineering thinking, design thinking and systems thinking (again with reference to projects in those disciplines).

Some authors have clearly recognised that the forms of disciplinary approach they are interested in (whether that is just one or a few) can be related to others, each of which has its own literature. However, note that although these various works compare different disciplinary approaches, they typically describe whatever collection of approaches they are engaging with as though they form some naturally occurring set, or the only set available. They don't indicate that they are looking at just one of many possible subsets. For example, Kelly and Gero (2021) describe design thinking and computational thinking as 'the only two forms of thinking to gain prominence since the turn of the 21st century' (p. 2), and Shin et al. (2022) say that to 'fully explain complex phenomena or solve problems using models requires both systems thinking (ST) and computational thinking (CT)' (p. 933). There are seemingly very few examples where disciplinary approaches are described not as a small, bounded set, but as a general class that is (or can be) populated with contributions from almost any discipline. Perhaps the clearest exception to this is found in the epilogue of Denning and Tedre's (2019) book on computational thinking, where they point out that

> everyone thinks their own field's ways of thinking (and practicing) are valuable and worthy of learning in many other fields. Enthusiasts want to spread the gospel of success to other fields. The list of 'thinkings' to be spread is long: computational thinking, logical thinking, economic thinking, systems thinking, physics thinking, mathematical thinking, engineering thinking, design thinking, ... and more (p. 213).

Denning and Tedre do not then analyse or compare these various disciplinary approaches or the projects they originate from, but they do acknowledge that variety, which is seemingly very rare.[18] In fact, just conducting simple literature

---

[18] Also see Rapoport's (2002) discussion of how the legal education system aims to train students in thinking like a lawyer: 'Why are we so fixated on the "thinking" process, rather than the "doing" process? No one expects a doctor to "think" like a doctor when she leaves medical school. We expect her to be a doctor. The same is true of those who have been trained as engineers, research scientists, car mechanics, and air traffic controllers. ... Even the most abstract philosopher "does" something in addition to "thinking": he publishes his thoughts and tentative conclusions in a way that furthers the discourse of philosophy' (pp. 92–93).

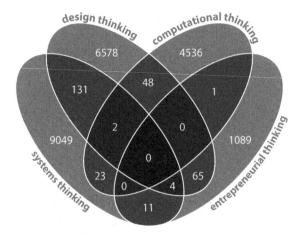

Figure 3 Illustration of the relative prominence of four forms of disciplinary approach in the scientific literature, both in terms of when they are referred to in isolation and when they are referred to in combination. The numbers represent the count of documents returned when searching the Scopus database for each term using Boolean operators (title, abstract and keywords from 1954 until the search date of February 2023). See online Appendix B for the underlying data.

searches for works on disciplinary approaches reveals the very small number of those works that focus on two or more approaches in comparison to those that focus on just one approach (see Figure 3). Similarly, it can be observed that even the most cited works describing one disciplinary approach (e.g. Wing's description of computational thinking) are seldom cited in works describing other disciplinary approaches (e.g. various descriptions of design thinking) (see online Appendix B, available at www.cambridge.org/Crilly).

6.2 Are These Approaches Really Discipline-Specific?

There is a duality at the centre of discussions about disciplinary approaches. On the one hand, these are approaches that are claimed to be discipline-specific: they characterise the particular disciplines that give them their names (e.g. *design* thinking). On the other hand, these are approaches that are claimed to be discipline-neutral: they have potentially wide-ranging application elsewhere (e.g. design thinking *in business,* or *in healthcare* or *in education*). One way to understand this duality is to view each approach as originating from a particular discipline, capturing its distinctive features, while also recognising that many other disciplines will also require or exhibit some or all of those features.[19] Using design as an example again, we could say that central to design is the practice of conceiving plans for enabling goal-directed change. When described at this level of abstraction, aspects of design thinking will clearly be employed in other disciplines, such as when scientists plan experiments to test hypotheses ('experiment design'). On the other hand, central to science is the practice of undertaking investigative activities that provide new insights about the world. When described at this level of abstraction, scientific thinking will clearly be employed in other disciplines, such as when designers conduct research to better understand potential users ('user research'). However, although scientists engage in design activities and designers engage in research activities, it needn't be that design approaches are thought to be characteristic of science, or that scientific approaches are thought to be characteristic of design (for design-science comparisons, see Crilly, 2010; Farrell & Hooker, 2013; Galle & Kroes, 2014).

Recognising that disciplinary approaches can be applied beyond their disciplinary origins raises an important question: once a disciplinary approach has been abstracted from its discipline-specific practices, transferred to another domain and then adapted to suit that domain, does it still carry the distinctive signature of the original discipline? For example, note that many discussions of design thinking look like earlier and ongoing discussions of a more discipline-neutral approach to creative problem solving (e.g. see Treffinger et al., 2006).[20] More generally, if disciplinary approaches are abstracted from disciplinary specifics, what exactly is it that makes the approach still disciplinary? Another way of thinking about this is to ask what characterises disciplines, what distinguishes them from each other, and how the described disciplinary approaches reflect those characteristics and distinctions.

Although I do not intend to get into a detailed discussion of disciplines here, it is worth noting that they are seemingly difficult to define (see Krishnan, 2009; Shumway & Messer-Davidow, 1991), perhaps as difficult as the associated

---

[19] This connects to the general notion of asking which skills are domain-general and which are domain-specific. As Christensen et al. (2023) recently observed in their comparison of design and entrepreneurship, '[o]nly by understanding how trained designers have both skills and abilities that stand out from other professions, as well as having skills and abilities that are found in other professions, will we be able to understand fully the roles that designers believe they can play – and intend to play – in design and elsewhere' (p. 18). The same applies to the other disciplines we are considering here.

[20] This is perhaps not surprising given the overlapping origins of these two approaches, with one (CPS) maintaining discipline-neutrality from the outset, and the other (design thinking) starting as discipline-specific before becoming more generalised. For example, in the 1950s and 1960s, Arnold's work at Stanford on creativity, education and innovation was influenced by Osborn's work on brainstorming and appeared in edited works by Parnes (see Auernhammer & Roth, 2021, pp. 631, 639).

approaches have proven to be! However, at a very general level, Chandler (2009) tells us that most meanings of discipline 'involve some notion of submission to a regularized set of practices, a sense of an imposed ordering of life and thought, body and mind' (p. 732). This meaning of disciplines is clearly connected to the kind of thing that we are considering disciplinary approaches to be, and reflects why they are each thought to be distinctive. A common way to consider such distinctions between disciplines is to classify them into a hierarchy, dividing them according to their subject matter, origins, objectives or something else. For example, notwithstanding the overlaps between academic and professional disciplines,[21] the former are often classified according to the structure of university departments (Chandler, 2009), while the latter are often classified according to the structure of professional associations (Greenwood et al., 2002). Despite this apparent order, disciplines are fragmented, heterogeneous and dynamic and interact with other disciplines in many complex ways (for discussions of the fluidity of disciplinary boundaries, see Gieryn, 1983). As a result, an overly strict conception of disciplinary boundaries sometimes prevents people from seeing the close connections that might be made across disciplines (Krishnan, 2009). This is something that a well-coordinated cross-discipline project to understand disciplinary approaches could address.

Looking at the various projects to define different disciplinary approaches, it is clear that in some cases particular components appear to be characteristic of many different disciplines. For example, 'problem solving' is listed as a component of design thinking (Micheli et al., 2019), computational thinking (Weintrop et al., 2016) and scientific thinking (Dunbar & Fugelsang, 2005). Similarly, 'empathy' appears as a component of both design thinking (Schweitzer et al., 2016) and anthropological thinking (Tett, 2021), while 'experimentation' appears as a component of both design thinking (Micheli et al., 2019) and entrepreneurial thinking (Frederiksen & Brem, 2017). Such overlaps between disciplinary approaches are easy to identify when the components are conveniently named and defined in near-identical ways. However, many more overlaps can be identified when we include the components that are named differently but where their definitions refer to very similar concepts. For example, the 'experimentation' component referred to above might also be closely related to 'being iterative and incremental' in computational thinking (Kong, 2019) or to 'hypothesis testing' in scientific thinking (Dunbar & Fugelsang, 2005).[22]

---

[21] See the earlier terminology discussion.

[22] Exploring wider associations like this encourages a search for sets of components that would collectively make up a unified practice. For example, the 'problem solving' components of approaches such as design, computational and scientific thinking might complement the

Even the components of disciplinary approaches that we might expect to be quite domain-specific can be found in other disciplines. For example, in evolutionary thinking, one of the three main components is 'tree thinking' which involves recognising that the shared characteristics of members of a group are determined by their descent from common ancestors. In studies of biological evolution, this involves thinking of species within the context of a phylogenetic tree, where branching occurs at distinct evolutionary events. However, as O'Hara (1997) notes in his description of one component of evolutionary thinking

> Although tree thinking as I have described it is an aspect of systematic biology, the idea of tree thinking isn't necessarily tied to living things – all it requires is descent and inheritance. A fascinating inorganic example of tree thinking can be found in a recent paper on the motion of asteroids (Milani & Farinella 1994), an example which makes use of many of the same ideas I have just outlined. (p. 325)

Indeed, Milani and Farinella (1994) are describing work on 'asteroid families', a group of asteroids that share similar motion characteristics (for billions of years) because they are descended from a single 'parent body' that was broken up in a past collision. This group of fragments are said to have 'inherited' the motion characteristics of that parent in a process of 'collisional evolution' (see Nesvorný et al., 2005). Of course, viewing diverse systems through the lens of biological evolution is widespread, including in discussions of cultural evolution (Lewens, 2015), technical evolution (Arthur, 2009), ideational evolution (Crilly, 2021b) and organisational evolution (Breslin, 2016). However, that is not necessarily the same as adopting and applying the thinking exhibited by evolutionary biologists. For example, one might observe certain similarities between how biological species and commercial organisations change over time – *and draw analogies on that basis* – without necessarily thinking about those organisations in the way that an evolutionary biologist would.

As we have seen, the components of one disciplinary approach can map to identical or similar components of other disciplinary approaches. That's quite straightforward, but things are more complicated when a component of one disciplinary approach seems to map to a whole other disciplinary approach, rather than just to a component of that other approach. For example, 'systems thinking' appears as just one component of entrepreneurial thinking

---

components of related approaches such as 'problem framing' in design thinking (Wrigley et al., 2021) and 'problem finding' in engineering thinking (Lucas et al., 2014). Of course, many of the disciplines discussed here engage in coordinated practices of problem finding, problem framing and problem solving, even if no project has represented these as a full set of components or integrated them into a single component.

(e.g. Grimes & Vogus, 2021), computational thinking (e.g. Weintrop et al., 2016) and engineering thinking (e.g. Lucas et al., 2014; Waks et al., 2011). However, systems thinking is itself broken down into many different components by the various authors who describe that as a disciplinary approach in its own right (e.g. see Arnold & Wade, 2015; Capra & Luisi, 2014; Richmond, 1993). Conversely, on at least one account, systems thinking includes a component called 'scientific thinking' (Richmond, 2016), which, again, others describe as an entire disciplinary approach that can be divided into several components (e.g. see Dunbar & Fugelsang, 2005; Noll, 1935).

Because one disciplinary approach might seemingly appear as a component of another disciplinary approach, these approaches might be considered at different levels of granularity. For example, entrepreneurial thinking can be divided into many components, one of which is, say, 'systems thinking' (Grimes & Vogus, 2021), and systems thinking can itself be divided into many components, one of which is, say, 'recognizing interconnections' (Arnold & Wade, 2015). We might then ask what a component like 'recognizing interconnections' can be further divided into (at a finer level of granularity), and also what 'entrepreneurial thinking' might be a component of (at a courser level). Such an investigation might aim at generating a large hierarchical structure where something like 'thinking' is at the coarsest level of granularity, and this is progressively broken down further and further. An alternative to this hierarchical view of disciplinary approaches is a network view (for a discussion of hierarchical and networked organisational structures, see Fischer, 2016). In this conception, the various ways of thinking constitute a space of possibilities, and disciplinary approaches are defined by how they connect through that space, linking different components into a coherent and descriptive set. One discipline's approach might be just a component of another discipline's approach, but disciplinary approaches in general would be defined by their full set of components and how those components are related. Including or overlapping with other disciplines would be permitted or encouraged, but perhaps most importantly, it would be acknowledged (we'll return to that later).

Attention to commonalities between the disciplinary approaches should not mask the fact that many of these approaches seemingly have components that are quite distinctive, common to only small sets of disciplines or perhaps even unique to one of them. For example, design thinking's reference to 'abductive reasoning' is quite unusual (e.g. Kimbell, 2011; Micheli et al., 2019), as is the principle of 'affordable loss' in entrepreneurial thinking (Sarasvathy, 2009), and also the focus on 'understanding feedback' in systems thinking (Arnold & Wade, 2015). These are unlike the components in any of the other disciplinary approaches reviewed here, but it is not clear whether this reveals genuinely unique features of these approaches, accidental omissions in the projects describing other disciplinary approaches or attention to different levels of description in those other projects. For example, although the design thinking project is perhaps the only such project to claim a special place for abduction, that mode of thought has been described as central to medical reasoning (V. L. Patel et al., 2005, p. 730) and legal practice (Askeland, 2020).[23] However, it is still the case that when each discipline's components are taken as a set, they are collectively distinctive and characteristic, despite some partial overlap with individual components of other disciplines.

6.3 Are These Approaches Really Transferrable?

In the previous section, I began by outlining the dual claims that are apparent or implicit in many accounts of disciplinary approaches: each one is both discipline-specific (in its origins) and yet discipline-neutral (in its potential application). Having now considered the issue of discipline-specificity, I turn to the issue of discipline-neutrality.

As we have seen, the various projects to define disciplinary approaches typically abstract away those aspects of the discipline that are thought to be overly specific. This is done with the goal of representing the transferrable essence of those disciplines' approaches, approaches that seemingly might be applied by almost anyone to almost anything. This is a tempting proposition because it suggests that a wide range of people can then learn to think like, say, a designer, an entrepreneur or an ecologist by learning just about each discipline's 'thinking' rather than undertaking training in the discipline itself.[24] Given that the learners' domains of application are likely to be very different to the domains traditionally associated with the approach they are training in, this might seem to provide a shortcut that is not just convenient but also justified. However, just how is it that practitioners acquire and develop the approaches that are taken to characterise their discipline? What is lost when discipline-specific factors such as subject matter are stripped away from descriptions of a discipline's practices? Such questions are seldom addressed by the projects that promote each disciplinary approach, and we would have to look elsewhere for clues.

Disciplinary styles are reported to be 'imprinted' on people by the 'signature pedagogies' of their academic and professional training, and by their early

---

[23] Note that while different modes of reasoning (such as induction, deduction and abduction) might be distinguished from each other for the purpose of analysis, they needn't be psychologically distinct in practice (for arguments and counterarguments, see Evans & Over, 2013).

[24] For example, referring to design thinking, Martin says that 'today's business people don't need to understand designers better, they need to become designers' (Dunne & Martin, 2006, p. 513).

professional experiences (Shulman, 2005; Blackwell et al., 2010). As such, the approaches that are practiced and promoted by each discipline might be thought to originate in those disciplines' distinctive histories, goals, values, materials, subjects, techniques, cultures, achievements and failures. This would suggest that attempts to extract disciplinary approaches from the originating disciplines could rob those approaches of the very characteristics that make them coherent and valuable. We might reasonably ask to what extent the various disciplinary approaches can be understood, acquired and developed without learners' involvement in the actual disciplines themselves. Is each discipline, in fact, the best place to learn the disciplinary approaches that they promote? Specifically, are those approaches best acquired and practised by working with each discipline's motivations, problems, materials, processes, constraints and specific forms of feedback? For example, are the components of design thinking best learnt by practicing architecture, product design or service design (for a discussion of such issues, see Kolko, 2018)? Or, is systems thinking best learnt by modelling the behaviour of natural ecosystems (for a related experiment, see Riess & Mischo, 2010)? We could go on through any list of disciplines that interest us asking similar questions about which experiences really shape the way practitioners develop and refine their disciplinary approaches. Those people who have been immersed in the specifics of a discipline's practices might be able to abstract from those specifics to recognise their own disciplinary approach and apply it elsewhere. However, we might wonder whether people from outside the discipline can be effectively trained just in the approaches and then meaningfully progress from such abstractions to new specifics that are relevant to them in their own domain (for a discussion of how teachers aim to encourage 'disciplinary patterns of language and thought', see Langer et al., 1993).

The various projects to define disciplinary approaches don't offer much guidance on the issues raised above, but another set of projects has: those defining *higher-order thinking skills*. Perhaps the most prominent of these skills is 'critical thinking', with associated work investigating how such thinking can be effectively taught, both within disciplines and independent of them (e.g. Halpern & Sternberg, 2020). However, there are also similar discussions of other forms of thinking that aren't tied to any specific discipline. A list of these higher-order thinking skills might include

- *'critical thinking'* (cited above);
- *'creative thinking'* (e.g. Webster, 1990);
- *'inventive thinking'* (e.g. Sokol et al., 2008);
- *'visual thinking'* (e.g. McKim, 1980);
- *'analogical thinking'* (e.g. Gentner & Maravilla, 2018);

- *'possibilistic thinking'* (e.g. Clarke, 2008);
- *'possibility thinking'* (e.g. Craft, 2015);
- *'futures thinking'* (e.g. A. Jones et al., 2012);
- *'flexible thinking'* (e.g. Barak & Levenberg, 2016);
- *'reflective thinking'* (e.g. Rodgers, 2002);
- *'open-minded thinking'* (e.g. Stanovich & West, 1997);
- *'model-based thinking'* (e.g. Warton et al., 2015);
- *'causal thinking'* (e.g. Illari et al., 2011).

Many of these general thinking skills are themselves subdivided into components (e.g. see Ennis, 1964), and they are also sometimes compared to each other (e.g. see Donald, 2002; Hitchcock, 2020).[25] In educational contexts, these skills are usually described in terms of 'teaching thinking', as opposed to teaching subject matter content (Wegerif, 2007, chs. 6–7; Wegerif et al., 2015), and so also share that feature with the disciplinary approaches we have been considering here.

Even a brief survey of the higher-order thinking skills shows that they overlap with the components of the disciplinary approaches. However, I'll focus here on critical thinking because it has one of the most well-established literatures (developed over several decades) and because that literature has explicitly addressed the issue of discipline-neutrality and the challenge of transfer. Although definitions vary, critical thinking is often associated with evaluating claims, assessing evidence, considering alternatives, employing logic and remaining sceptical.[26] However, just as we have seen that disciplinary approaches include not just thinking skills, but also knowledge, attitudes, habits and dispositions, the same is true for critical thinking. To quote Halpern and Sternberg (2020), critical thinking is 'the willingness to engage in and persist at a complex task, demonstrate flexible and openminded thinking, and the readiness to abandon non-productive strategies and self-correct when needed' (p. 3).

In whatever ways it might be defined, critical thinking is widely regarded as an essential approach across a wide range of disciplines and is the stated objective of education at many levels (e.g. see Willingham, 2007). Because so many different disciplines value and promote critical thinking, it has often been described as though it is a single set of skills and inclinations that can be applied in different contexts. This has led to the creation of general critical thinking

---

[25] For works that collect some of these forms of thinking together, see (Ball & Thompson, 2018; Cummins, 2021; Holyoak & Morrison, 2005).

[26] Note that just as work engaging with disciplinary approaches has complained about inconsistent and vague definitions, so has work engaging with general higher-order thinking skills (e.g. for such complaints about critical thinking, see McPeck, 1981, ch1). Similar ambiguities surround Dewey's earlier concept of reflective thinking (Rodgers, 2002).

courses, which aim to teach critical thinking separately from disciplinary subject matter. The idea is that these courses develop widely applicable critical thinking skills that can later be demonstrated in any number of subjects, ranging from philosophy and literature to mathematics and the natural sciences. However, analysis of these courses and their performance has led other people to argue that critical thinking is really just an umbrella term for sets of skills and inclinations that vary greatly according to the specific contexts of application (for summaries of the debates, see Ennis, 1964, 1989; McPeck, 1981, 1990; Moore, 2011). As Sternberg (2020) points out

> Probably anyone who has taken advanced courses in, say, physics and litera-
> ture, has observed that although both may require critical thinking, the kinds
> of critical thinking are different across the disciplines, at least as they are
> usually practiced. One can use the same label, 'critical thinking,' to refer to
> serious, reflective thinking in each of these areas, but the labels do not
> necessarily describe the same thing. (p. 320).

Observations like Sternberg's have led to proposals that critical thinking is not a separate, widely applicable skill, but is something that should be taught within disciplines, applied to the subject matter that is most relevant. One consequence of the apparent discipline-specificity of critical thinking is the difficulties that people experience when they are required to take critical thinking concepts or skills from one domain and apply them to another. There then seems to be a tendency for critical thinking learnt in one domain to become 'attached' to the problems that are seen in that domain, rather than being freely and effectively transferred to other kinds of problems (for an analysis of this with respect to professional practice, see Lilienfeld et al., 2020; for an analysis of this with respect to education, see Willingham, 2007, 2019). The relevant literature does not conclude that training in critical thinking is impossible, but certainly challenging. The notion of transfer is key, and it is advised that educational courses are explicitly designed to encourage transfer, including demonstrations of discipline specificity and neutrality (e.g. see Halpern & Sternberg, 2020; Perkins & Salomon, 1989; Willingham, 2007).

Critical thinking is directly relevant to many disciplinary approaches, either because critical thinking is a component of those approaches, or because those approaches are a specialised application of critical thinking. For example, Schweitzer et al. (2016) include critical thinking as a component of design thinking, Noll (1935) includes it as a component of scientific thinking and Ruggiero (1996) includes it as a component of sociological thinking. Conversely, Willingham (2007) regards such disciplinary approaches as differ-ent forms of critical thinking, saying 'there are specific types of critical thinking that are characteristic of different subject matter: That's what we mean when we refer to "thinking like a scientist" or "thinking like a historian"' (p. 8; also see Sternberg, 2020). So, some people regard critical thinking as a part of certain disciplinary approaches, whereas others regard disciplinary approaches as specific forms of critical thinking. Either way, critical thinking is intertwined with many of the disciplinary approaches, and the same could be said of the other higher-order thinking skills, each of which also has a body of literature associated with it. These literatures have typically been overlooked in discussions of disciplinary approaches, even though they address many overlapping themes, including education and transfer. A closer integration of research on disciplinary approaches and the higher-order thinking skills would be beneficial, especially for our understanding of how to educate for transfer between domains. For a rare example of this, see English's (2023) work on different ways of thinking in problem solving, which includes a focus on critical thinking, systems thinking and design thinking.

Many of the projects to define particular disciplinary approaches make claims for their general applicability: apparently, everyone can benefit from thinking like a designer, or like an ecologist, entrepreneur, computer scientist, and so on. However, for this to be true requires effective transfer from the originating discipline to the domain of application. A relevant consideration here is how far something is being transferred, either in terms of the distance between disciplines or application domains (for a taxonomy of transfer distances, see Barnett & Ceci, 2002). For example, a recent meta-analysis of transfer effects from teaching computer programming found positive effects for activities close to computing (near transfer: creative thinking, mathematical skills and metacognition), whereas activities further from computing benefitted the least (far transfer: school achievement and literacy) (Scherer et al., 2019). Clearly, if the claims about the wide applicability of disciplinary approaches are to be supported, then courses (or other interventions) will need to be developed with this in mind, and studies will need to be conducted to assess their effectiveness in this regard (e.g. see Carlgren et al., 2016; Kurtmollaiev et al., 2018). Adopting such a focus on transfer has implications not just for how the interventions should be evaluated, but also how they should be designed so that such assessment is possible (e.g. for this argument applied to systems thinking training, see Cavaleri & Sterman, 1997).

It should be acknowledged here that considering higher-order thinking skills (e.g. critical thinking) might make us question the distinction between these skills and the many disciplinary approaches that we have been focussed on (e.g. design thinking). On the one hand, each disciplinary approach might originate from specific professional practices or academic traditions. On the other hand, higher-order thinking skills might be more general and remain independent of any such practices or traditions. This sort of distinction might be easiest to defend when the disciplinary approaches under consideration are like design thinking, entrepreneurial thinking and computational thinking. These approaches are derived from the work of designers, entrepreneurs and computer scientists, each of whom is associated with specific professional practices and academic traditions. However, what about something like systems thinking, which I have so far treated as a disciplinary approach? If the term 'systems thinking' describes how systems biologists or systems engineers think, then perhaps it is indeed *disciplinary*. However, if systems thinking is instead described as a discipline-neutral approach then it might just as well be treated as a higher-order thinking skill rather than anything disciplinary. In fact, instead of being a special case, systems thinking is just a clear illustration of the problem of trying to classify any of these ways of thinking. If a disciplinary approach originates in a discipline but is then abstracted for wide-ranging application elsewhere then perhaps it has become a general higher-order thinking skill (or a set of such skills). Perhaps all disciplinary approaches are actually just higher-order thinking skills, rather than being disciplinary after all. These two overarching categories might really just be two ends of a continuum, with some ways of thinking seeming to be more attached to disciplines and others seeming to be more detached from them.

6.4 What about Sub-disciplines and Inter-disciplines?

With all this talk of discipline specificity and neutrality, it makes sense to consider exactly what is included and excluded within the bounds of any particular discipline. However, the various projects to define disciplinary approaches have typically been phrased in very general terms that cover large disciplines, and therefore – *implicitly* – many sub-disciplines. For example, discussions of design thinking generally do not distinguish the approaches used in product design from those used in engineering design or software design, and yet also do not explicitly claim that these sub-disciplines are all united by the same overall approach. We might ask whether components such as 'developing empathy' or 'iterative prototyping' are equally important in each sub-discipline of design. Similar questions could be asked about many other disciplinary approaches:

- *'Systems thinking'* – is this describing the approach taken by those working in ecology, systems biology or systems engineering?
- *'Entrepreneurial thinking'* – is this describing the approach taken by those working on technology-related or service-related ventures?
- *'Computational thinking'* – is this describing the approach taken by those working in information systems, software engineering or computer networks?

Distinctions like these could be identified within all the other disciplines for which disciplinary approaches have been defined: 'geographical thinking' (human or physical?), 'scientific thinking' (natural or social?), 'economic thinking' (model-based or heterodox?), and so on. Whatever discipline we consider, it can be divided further and further into sub-disciplines and sub-sub-disciplines. Those divisions might be made on the basis of subject matter knowledge, applied techniques, or just, well, . . . on the basis of some general *approach*. As such, interpreting claims made about a single overarching disciplinary approach, such as design thinking, requires some caution. This is because we don't know if those claims apply to any or all of the sub-disciplines we might be interested in.

An alternative interpretation of the projects to define disciplinary approaches is that they are not really identifying the overarching approaches that are common to all their many sub-disciplines. Instead, perhaps they are – *again implicitly* – prioritising just one or some of the sub-disciplines but giving the approach a much more general name. For example, is design thinking really more like *product* design thinking or *service* design thinking? The examples that are often used to illustrate the sources of design thinking might suggest that it is one of these that is dominant (but also see Pressman, 2018; Wrigley et al., 2021). Additionally, is it Western perspectives and practices that are taken to be central to design thinking, or are those from other regions equally represented (for discussions of African design thinking, see Ambole, 2020)? More generally, just whose design are we talking about when we talk about design thinking, who decides that, how is that decision made and how do we know? Similar questions can be asked for systems thinking, entrepreneurial thinking and for all the other disciplinary approaches considered here (e.g. for discussions of indigenous worldviews relevant to systems thinking, see Goodchild, 2021; Spiller et al., 2020).

A more transparent way of describing each discipline's approach might be to start by identifying the various sub-disciplines (and other variants) of relevance: what distinguishes them and how are they related? We could then identify the distinct approaches that characterise each sub-discipline and the common approaches that characterise the discipline as a whole. Some of these common approaches might be shared by many or all sub-disciplines; some might be shared by only a few; some sub-disciplines might have specialised approaches that are not shared with the overall discipline, or with many or any of the other sub-disciplines. In considering things in this way, we should note that parts of two completely different disciplines might actually be more similar to each other than two very different parts of the same discipline (Becher, 2017, ch. 2). For example, consider the broad discipline of engineering, which might include

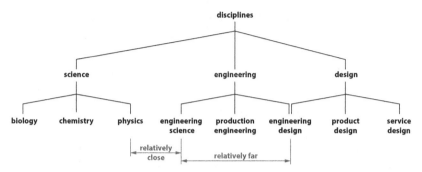

Figure 4 Diagram showing (i) how sub-disciplinary approaches of different disciplines (in this case engineering and science) might be more similar than sub-disciplinary approaches of the same discipline (engineering), and (ii) how inter-disciplines (like *engineering design*) might exhibit characteristics of two or more disciplines (like engineering *and* design).

sub-disciplines of engineering science and engineering design.[27] *The approach taken in engineering science* might be closer to scientific thinking than it is to design thinking. In contrast, *the approach taken in engineering design* might be closer to design thinking than scientific thinking (for related discussions, see Dzombak & Beckman, 2020; Waks et al., 2011). See Figure 4 for an illustration of these issues, and as a possible partial expansion of Figure 1. Perhaps more accurate – but also more complex – is the idea that disciplinary relations should be considered as a network rather than a hierarchy, where all disciplines and sub-disciplines are related to each other in some way (see Figure 3 in Rosvall & Bergstrom, 2011).

As indicated in Figure 4, some sub-disciplines, such as engineering design, lie at the intersection of two or more disciplines, and thus might 'inherit' common approaches from two or more 'parents'. Another example is synthetic biology, which is a hybrid of biological science and engineering, and draws from both disciplines. Practitioners of synthetic biology might thus be expected to employ forms of biological thinking and engineering thinking, while possibly also exhibiting approaches that are not found in either (see discussions in Endy, 2005; Knight, 2005). For our purposes here, perhaps the most prominent discussion of such inter-disciplines is 'systemic design', which is described as a disciplinary approach in its own right, one which is divided into several components (for a review, see Kaur & Craven, 2020, pp. 202–205). However,

---

[27] These divisions and further divisions of knowledge might be thought of as consistent with the 'fractal model' of expertise, where the structure is essentially the same at each level (Collins, 2018, p. 70).

there are many of these inter-disciplines, the practices of which might be expected to combine characteristics of two or more of the approaches that we have been considering, and others too (for a framework of options, see McComb & Jablokow, 2022).

In addition to considering disciplines, sub-disciplines and inter-disciplines, there are other ways in which disciplinary approaches might be divided. For example, Denning and Tedre (2021; also see Tedre & Denning, 2022) distinguish between computational thinking for beginners and computational thinking for professionals, arguing that the approaches of each group are different, or at least that the challenges they engage with are.[28] This is unusual, and just as projects to define disciplinary approaches generally do not engage with sub-disciplines, they also generally do not engage with levels of expertise or other such forms of distinction. However, whether divided by sub-disciplinary specialisation, expertise level or something else, considering discipline decomposition and comparison might not conform to the overall goal of representing disciplinary approaches in a way that is accessible to outsiders. Still, it might provide a more nuanced basis from which such accessible representations can be constructed, and it might also permit more transparency for those seeking to understand the foundations of claims that are seemingly made about entire disciplines.

Considering the different ways in which disciplines can be decomposed and combined might prompt us to reconsider the utility of categorising approaches according to disciplines after all. On the one hand, categorisation according to traditional disciplinary categories can seem inevitable because those disciplines have long been reified as a way to divide up knowledge, learning and practice (Greenwood et al., 2002; Chandler, 2009). It is also within those disciplines that the projects to define disciplinary approaches have taken place, and it is after those disciplines that the approaches are named. On the other hand, we have seen that definitions of disciplinary approaches are typically presented at a level of abstraction that strips away many of the discipline's details to emphasise their transferrable essence. For people outside the discipline seeking to apply that approach to their own work, we might question whether it should really interest them which discipline the approach originated from. For example, if someone in an organisation wants to implement some innovative change to how a business

---

[28] The components they list for beginners include 'abstraction', 'problem decomposition' and 'simulation'. Some of their components for professionals are also descriptions of modes of thought (or things thought about)—*but presumably now more advanced*—including design patterns, pattern recognition, concurrency and non-determinism. However, some of these professional computational thinking components seemingly refer to technologies, such as bytecode and virtual machines (Tedre & Denning, 2022, p. 3).

process is managed, does it matter whether an iterative low-fidelity build-and-test technique is imported from design, engineering, computer science, entrepreneurship or somewhere else? Does it matter where they think that approach has come from, or even if they think it has come from anywhere other than the domain they are from, such as management?

If we answer the questions with a 'yes', then we assert that disciplinary identity is an important part of disciplinary approaches, even though that is not what the projects to define such approaches have emphasised. With their focus on abstraction, each project instead emphasises the components that make up their own particular disciplinary approach, but not on what associations people make with that discipline, or what the naming of the approach means to those people. However, although something like design thinking might be usefully decomposed into a set of components that can be individually learnt, developed and applied, perhaps what is more important is that learners recognise that the problem they are addressing *is a design problem*, that they are engaged *in design activities* and that they are acting *as designers*. Similarly, the components of entrepreneurial thinking might mean less to learners than the idea that they should *be entrepreneurial or act like an entrepreneur*, even if they are not launching a new business venture, but perhaps just operating within an established organisation (for a discussion of intrapreneurial thinking, see Sayeed & Gazdar, 2003). The same might be said of many other disciplinary approaches, where emphasis could be placed on thinking and acting like a forest ecologist (systems thinking), a software engineer (computational thinking), and so on. To be clear, the distinction here is between emphasising the particularities of the disciplinary practice (or part of it) rather than eradicating such details in the interests of codification and generalisation.

If instead we think that disciplinary origins are not important to the promotion of disciplinary approaches (answering those earlier questions with a 'no'), then we might look for alternative categorisations of the approaches that have previously been associated with specific disciplines. These new categories of practice would either be independent of traditional disciplines or would place them in higher-level categories. For example, individual disciplines might be grouped according to whether they are investigative, artistic, social or enterprising (Smart et al., 2009, p. 489), or according to any of the many other schemes of discipline grouping (for a review, see W. A. Jones, 2011, p. 11). Such moves might then emphasise things like 'investigative thinking', which could include many components that are currently distributed across a wide range of disciplinary approaches from the natural and social sciences. Alternatively, we could focus not on the disciplines (whether traditional or newly defined) but instead on the finer-grained components of practice from which they are made up. This might, for example, shift the emphasis to approaches like 'prototype thinking' or 'pivot thinking', rather than the disciplines that exhibit those practices (perhaps design and entrepreneurship). However, we might question whether prototype thinking or pivot thinking would each be just one type of thing, or whether they would vary substantially across disciplines and sub-disciplines, as has been found for critical thinking (for related work on visualisation, see Eckert et al., 2012). Another example might be 'complexity thinking' (e.g. see McCool et al., 2015; Richardson, 2008), which can be divided into different components, and where the weighting of those components can be seen to vary between sub- or inter-disciplines, such as swarm robotics and synthetic biology (Chen & Crilly, 2016).

As we can see, diverging from disciplinary classifications is not straightforward, and might involve giving up some clarity in a discussion that generally needs more of just that, not less. However, we should acknowledge that the existing focus on broad disciplinary approaches can mask important differences within disciplinary boundaries, and important commonalities across them.

7 Mapping Disciplinary Approaches to Each Other

We have seen that the different disciplinary approaches are interconnected and complementary, so anyone interested in one of them would likely be interested in others too. Mapping the approaches would therefore be beneficial, providing a visual guide to what the approaches are, and how they are related to each other. Although this is seldom done in the literature, when it is attempted, a Venn diagram is sometimes used to show that different approaches are overlapping but not identical. For example, Sneider et al. (2014, p. 11) present such an illustration of the intersection between mathematical thinking and computational thinking (at a component level), and Lewrick et al. (2018, p. 219) present a similarly structured illustration of the intersection between design thinking and systems thinking. If we are just considering the overall approaches for the three disciplines that I have most emphasised here, then the corresponding diagram might look something like Figure 5.[29]

Rather than something precise, Figure 5 is really just an indication of how we might visualise the relationships between three disciplinary approaches. Other perspectives on any of those approaches – *or shifts in emphasis about them* – would change how the sets are labelled, and also the intersections. Figure 5 also doesn't offer much detail, and there are clearly aspects of each approach that are

---

[29] For a very different representation of the relations between the same three approaches, see the illustration offered by Patel and Mehta (2017, p. 525).

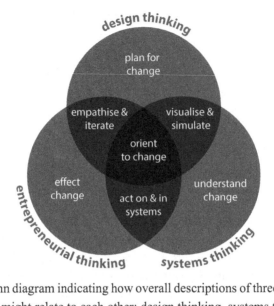

Figure 5 Venn diagram indicating how overall descriptions of three disciplinary approaches might relate to each other: design thinking, systems thinking and entrepreneurial thinking.

not represented. If we wanted a more complete representation, then we could add component lists to each part of the Venn diagram. In attempting to draw such a diagram, we would need to grapple with a number of problems that we have already noted:

- the components are all of different kinds, both within and across disciplines (e.g. some are ways of thinking, but some are seemingly habits, practices or capabilities);
- even components of the same kind are defined at different levels of abstraction (i.e. some are very general and others are quite specific);
- across disciplines, different terminology is used to describe the same thing (e.g. the same kind of thing might be meant by 'iteration', 'experimentation' and 'testing');
- also across disciplines, the same or similar terminology is used to describe quite different things (e.g. 'tree-by-tree thinking' and 'tree thinking' have no relation to each other).[30]

---

[30] In describing the components of systems thinking, Richmond (2016) compares holistic 'forest thinking' with analytic 'tree-by-tree thinking'. This tree-by-tree thinking is based on decomposition and individual analysis, examining things one by one. In contrast, and as explained earlier, in describing the components of evolutionary thinking it is common to use the term 'tree thinking' to describe a focus on descent and inheritance (e.g. see O'Hara, 1997).

All of this means that if each approach is to be described in its own terms, with the components that each discipline's project has defined, then it will be difficult to find shared components to represent in a Venn diagram. Such diagrams are also often sensibly limited to representing three or four sets before things become visually complex (for a discussion, see Mamakani & Ruskey, 2012). Another form of representation will be required if each disciplinary approach is to be described in its own terms, and if multiple approaches are to be mapped.

Despite the problems we might encounter, in some instances, one-to-one mappings can be identified between components from different disciplines, whether or not they are labelled with similar terms. Such mappings might indicate a clear correspondence, complementary perspectives or some more vague relationship. In other instances, one-to-many mappings can be identified, for example where a broadly specified component from one discipline can be related to various components from other disciplines (whatever kind of relationship this is). Just two illustrations of such possible mappings are offered here, to sketch out the kinds of options available. In Figure 6, a particular variant of *a single disciplinary approach* is taken to be of central interest, and its components are mapped to the components of several other disciplinary approaches (again, just a single variant in each case). In contrast, in Figure 7, *multiple disciplinary approaches* are taken to be of interest, and the components of each approach are aggregated from different variants, with these components mapped to the components of the other approaches. In both these figures, the approaches and variants that have been selected are just indicative, and others could be selected, depending on our interests and objectives.

Examining these two illustrations might raise all sorts of questions that are specifically about the relationships between the different disciplinary approaches that have been represented and the variants that have been selected. For example, considering Figure 6, we might ask whether these are the only disciplinary approaches to which design thinking should be related. What about scientific thinking, economic thinking, craft thinking, and so on? Or, looking at Figure 7, we might ask whether being creative is really only a component of design thinking and entrepreneurial thinking. What about systems thinking and computational thinking? Questions like these – *and many others that we might ask* – highlight that what we have here are not necessarily maps of how these disciplinary approaches are related to each other. Instead, they are only maps of how certain descriptions of them are related. However, note that I am putting these sketches forward here as an indication of the kinds of representation that it would be productive to construct if we could, not as definitive instances of such representations. Phrased another way, these sketches are not a solution to the

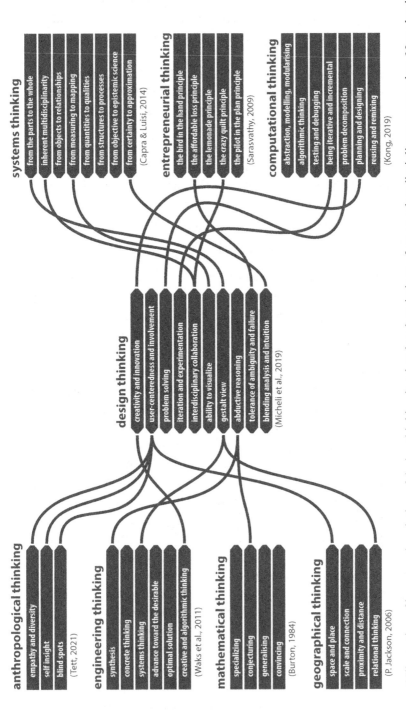

Figure 6 Illustration of how one description of design thinking is related to descriptions of seven other disciplinary approaches. Note that in this illustration, every component of design thinking is connected to a component of another approach. The arrangement of the disciplines is only for graphical clarity and is not otherwise meaningful. Definitions of each component for each variant can be found in Section 4.

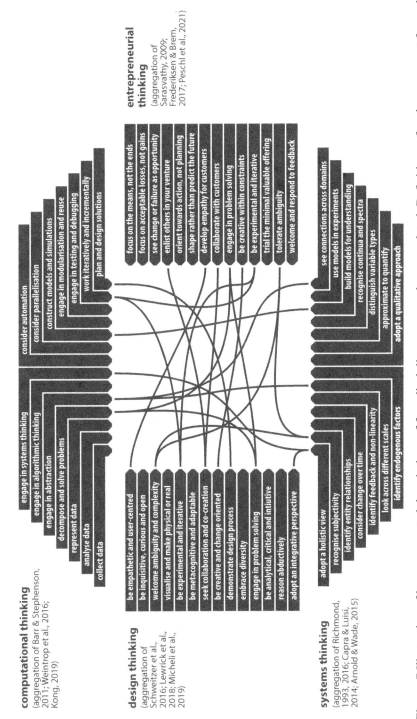

computational thinking
(aggregation of Barr & Stephenson, 2011; Weintrop et al., 2016; Kong, 2019)

- engage in systems thinking
- engage in algorithmic thinking
- engage in abstraction
- decompose and solve problems
- represent data
- analyse data
- collect data
- consider automation
- consider parallelisation
- construct models and simulations
- engage in modularisation and reuse
- engage in testing and debugging
- work iteratively and incrementally
- plan and design solutions

design thinking
(aggregation of Schweitzer et al., 2016; Lewrick et al., 2018; Micheli et al., 2019)

- be empathetic and user-centred
- be inquisitive, curious and open
- welcome ambiguity and complexity
- visualise and make physical or real
- be experimental and iterative
- be metacognitive and adaptable
- seek collaboration and co-creation
- be creative and change oriented
- demonstrate design process
- embrace diversity
- engage in problem solving
- be analytical, critical and intuitive
- reason abductively
- adopt an integrative perspective

entrepreneurial thinking
(aggregation of Sarasvathy, 2009; Frederiksen & Brem, 2017; Peschl et al., 2021)

- focus on the means, not the ends
- focus on acceptable losses, not gains
- see change or failure as opportunity
- enlist others in your venture
- orient towards action, not planning
- shape rather than predict the future
- develop empathy for customers
- collaborate with customers
- engage in problem solving
- be creative within constraints
- be experimental and iterative
- trial the minimal valuable offering
- tolerate ambiguity
- welcome and respond to feedback

systems thinking
(aggregation of Richmond, 1993, 2016; Capra & Luisi, 2014; Arnold & Wade, 2015)

- adopt a holistic view
- recognise subjectivity
- identify entity relationships
- consider change over time
- identify feedback and non-linearity
- look across different scales
- identify endogenous factors
- see connections across domains
- use models in experiments
- build models for understanding
- recognise continua and spectra
- distinguish variable types
- approximate to quantify
- adopt a qualitative approach

Figure 7 Illustration of how aggregated descriptions of four disciplinary approaches are related. Definitions of each component for each variant can be found in Section 4 and online Appendix C (where the aggregations are also illustrated).

problem of poor coordination across projects but are actually – when examined closely – revealing of the need for better coordination.

If the available descriptions of disciplinary approaches were explicitly comparative and were each constructed at the same level of analysis, then any sketches of the relationships between them might be more revealing of things we want to look at, and less revealing of the mutual isolation of the projects conducted to date. Rather than diving into the discipline- and variant-specific questions posed above, let's instead consider some more general questions, which I hope my problematic sketches motivate in a concrete way:

1. Which disciplines and sub-disciplines should be related?
2. Which variants of each discipline's approach should be included?
3. How should the disciplines or the components be ordered?
4. What kind of relationships should be shown or prioritised?
5. How should components of different kinds be related?
6. Should components be redefined for consistency?
7. How should disciplines be grouped or named?

If questions like these could be answered then a representation of the relationships between different disciplinary approaches could have many uses, either for research, education, training or practice. First, those interested in a particular disciplinary approach could be directed toward other related disciplinary approaches that include either similar or complementary components. Second, those interested in a particular component of a disciplinary approach could be directed toward the other disciplinary approaches that also include that component (see earlier discussion). Third, those interested in forming diverse groups could do so on the basis not just of demographic diversity (Gibbs et al., 2019), cognitive diversity (Mello & Rentsch, 2015) or functional diversity (Bunderson & Sutcliffe, 2002), but also according to some diversity in approach. For example, depending on context, groups could be formed to combine design, systems and entrepreneurial thinking, or to combine different approaches to something like iteration, which is important in many disciplines. While disciplinary approaches might be closely related to organisational function, these approaches have the benefit of being explicitly described in terms of their components, and might also vary within the same organisational function (e.g. if computer scientists and engineers both work within a 'technical' group). As such, mapping the relations between different group members' disciplinary approaches might help to make explicit, and thus combat, differences in their representation of the task being undertaken (for a discussion of these 'representational gaps', see Cronin & George, 2023).

Above are just some examples of how having a clearer map of the relationships between disciplinary approaches could assist research, education or application. With mapping like this as a proposed output of a more coordinated project (although not limited to the forms my illustrations take), I now explore some different methods by which such coordination might be achieved.

7.1 Will the Existing Literatures Suffice?

In considering various disciplinary approaches, I've here attempted to read across disciplinary boundaries and draw material together for comparison and synthesis. However, the many problems encountered in trying to do this constitute the bulk of what I have been describing. Such problems make the process of cross-disciplinary literature review very challenging, perhaps even more challenging than such reviews normally are (for methodological guidance see Cronin & George, 2023). To be clear, there are cross-disciplinary integrative reviews on relevant topics, including creativity and innovation (Acar et al., 2019), idea generation and selection (Hua et al., 2022), design and problem solving (Crilly, 2021a), and entrepreneurship (Ireland & Webb, 2007). It's just that these reviews have not focussed on disciplinary approaches, but rather on other factors relevant to the practices that take place within and across disciplines.

A different orientation to the published literatures would be a content analysis study, counting and examining references to different components of each approach across different disciplines. For example, if 'problem solving' is identified as a component of a specific disciplinary approach then that could provide the stimulus for searching other disciplines' literatures for that and related terms. The relevant bodies of work might include both the research literature and practitioner literature across a number of disciplines. This process could then be repeated for a range of different components, such as problem finding, problem framing, and so on. Such searches would permit analysis of the relevant weighting for each component in each discipline. Augmenting such a study with semantic analysis of the keyword occurrences would provide further context, either for sense checking a proportion of the data or for a more qualitative analysis (for an illustration of such an approach, see Roehling et al., 2000).

Although there are options for conducting a cross-disciplinary review of the existing literature, that will always involve working with what we've got, which in this case, might not be what we need. I think other methods will be required, methods that generate new data.

7.2 Can Experts Provide the Required Insights?

An alternative to seeking clarity in the published literatures on disciplinary approaches would be to survey the opinions of experts, explicitly seeking cross-disciplinary comparisons. Two categories of expert are easily identifiable, categories which might sometimes overlap.

First, there are researchers of disciplinary approaches, such as those who have published many of the works cited here: experts in the study of design thinking, systems thinking, entrepreneurial thinking, and so on. Although these researchers have seemingly mostly thought about their own disciplinary approaches in isolation, there are opportunities to address this: these researchers could be invited to define their disciplinary approach in relation to something else; they could be invited to reflect on the connections to closely allied disciplines; they could be asked to respond to the accounts of other disciplinary approaches. The application of such elicitation techniques could yield better definitions of the approach taken in each expert's own discipline and also new information about the relationships between disciplines. This might be even more effective where experts can be identified who have detailed knowledge of more than one disciplinary approach. Interactions between experts could be facilitated by reference to many of the lists, tables and diagrams that illustrate the description of individual disciplinary approaches or to comparative diagrams, such as the sketches in Figures 5, 6 and 7 (for descriptions of visual and verbal elicitation techniques, see Crilly et al., 2006; Ford & Sterman, 1998).

Second, in addition to researchers, the practitioners of each discipline could be surveyed for their opinions of the characteristics of their own approaches. This could involve assembling groups of practitioners from across a range of disciplines to discuss similarities and differences in their approaches. Alternatively, researchers could identify practitioners who have two or more disciplinary associations, either having moved between disciplines or combining two or more in their current practice. This would provide an opportunity for abstracting from the specifics of disciplinary practices in a comparative way. For an example of such an approach at the level of sub-disciplines, see Eckert et al.'s (2012) study of sketching in various branches of design, which identifies both common and distinct experiences with this form of visualisation. Although conducted with different objectives, it is also useful here to consider Strober's (2006, 2011) reports on a series of workshops with specialists in different academic disciplines. She describes participants learning to better understand their own disciplinary approaches when they saw those approaches contrasted with those of other participants. However, Strober's work also warns that such interactions might be challenging because of the very thing that is of interest:

the differing approaches of the participants make communication and coordination difficult, resulting in conflict (for advice on explicitly addressing this, see Strober, 2006, pp. 229–230).

7.3 How Can Cross-Discipline Practice be Observed?

As informative as published literature and expert opinion might be, the claims made about disciplinary approaches are generally about practices (not people's descriptions of those practices or their reflections on them) and about how those practices transfer to other domains (not what people claim about such transfer). Because of this, some more direct comparative study of disciplinary approaches in action would be valuable. To illustrate the potential for this, I outline just two possible kinds of study here.

First, researchers could define a set of discipline-neutral tasks to which various disciplinary approaches could be applied. Practitioners from those various disciplines are then set those tasks, with their approaches recorded for analysis. Researchers could subsequently work to identify any differences and commonalities in the approaches taken across disciplines. Whether practitioners were working individually or collaboratively, studies such as this would present opportunities to compare disciplinary approaches on the same terms, with the same tasks, same data and even with opportunities for analysis from different perspectives (e.g. psychological, sociological and educational). I don't find studies like this in the published literature, with most comparative studies of disciplines being based on comparisons of how each goes about its work within its normal context (e.g. see Becher, 2017). However, it should be noted that the kind of comparative studies I am suggesting might involve considerable methodological challenges, especially if the disciplinary differences do not just characterise the individuals and groups to be compared, but also influence the tasks that are relevant to those comparisons (for a general discussion of the challenges surrounding comparative studies of thinking, see Cole & Means, 1981, pp. 2, 11).

Second, and more naturalistically, researchers could identify practitioners who have two or more disciplinary associations, either having moved between disciplines, or combining two or more in their current practice. This would provide an opportunity for observing how those practitioners approach their work and distinguishing how those approaches compare with those of their more monodisciplinary colleagues. For example, if some practitioners had moved from the design domain to the policy domain, then researchers could study how those designers' approaches to policy work differed from the approaches demonstrated by their colleagues (for related case studies of the temporary transfer of designers into other sectors, see Wrigley et al., 2020). Alternatively, in sectors that draw from a wide range of disciplines (e.g. education, management consultancy), comparative studies could be conducted, investigating how those from different backgrounds approach the same kind of task. Again, I don't find comparative studies like this in the published literature, but the concepts of 'epistemic games' (Perkins, 1997) and 'epistemic fluency' (Goodyear & Markauskaite, 2017) might help with analysis of the data.

8 Reconsidering Disciplinary Approaches

As we have seen again and again, the different projects to define disciplinary approaches have been conducted in mutual isolation. Each discipline's approach has been described and promoted separately, with any distinctions or connections to other approaches seldom explored in detail. When other projects are acknowledged, this is almost always with reference to a small set of disciplines, without acknowledging that the general claims being made might apply to all disciplines. In any case, even these limited comparisons are quite rare, and the overwhelming majority of the literature describes individual disciplinary approaches in comparison to individual disciplinary practices: design thinking is compared to designing a product, entrepreneurial thinking is compared to founding a tech company, and so on. The focus is on the abstraction from these specific disciplinary practices, rather than on *what kind of thing* results from those abstractions (i.e. a form of disciplinary approach) and thus *what else it is related to* (i.e. other forms of disciplinary approach).

The mutual isolation of projects describing each disciplinary approach has resulted in fragmented accounts, inconsistent terminology, duplicated effort and compromised outputs.[31] The work required to define the different approaches and the components from which they are made up, would be greatly assisted by detailed reference to similar projects in other disciplines. This could take the form of sharing information on the goals of the projects, the methods by which the work is conducted, the format of the outputs and the ways in which those outputs are applied and tested. Recurring debates about the strengths and weaknesses of promoting any particular discipline's approach would be more productive if they were

---

[31] For a rare discussion of how the different projects should learn from each other, see Collopy (2019, p. 97): '"design thinking" ... will fail to have a lasting impact, unless we learn from the mistakes of earlier, related ideas. For instance, "systems thinking", which shares many of the conceptual foundations of "design thinking", promised to be a powerful guide to management practice, but it has never achieved the success its proponents hoped for'.

connected to similar ongoing debates in other disciplines, and to similar debates about higher-order thinking skills, such as critical thinking. More practically, the work of reforming education toward a focus on approaches (rather than subject matter content), or the packaging and delivery of related training content, would similarly benefit from sharing experiences across disciplines.

The challenges that arise when collecting and comparing a set of isolated discussions of specific disciplinary approaches should not distract from the value of those approaches. The widespread interest in things like design thinking, systems thinking or entrepreneurial thinking should be celebrated. It demonstrates that people recognise the limitations of their own habitual approaches, and the opportunities that lie in adopting approaches from other disciplines that they might otherwise neglect. The delivery of training in these approaches – and people's participation in that training – should also be celebrated. The successful formulation and application of this learning shows that people don't require full immersion in a discipline's history, materials and techniques to benefit from some of what characterises that discipline. Instead, such training offers individuals and groups an accessible route to expand the range of approaches available to them, focussing on what can be learnt and what can be applied across domains.

Despite all there is to celebrate about disciplinary approaches, a more coordinated project is required, one which will view each approach as a member of a larger set. By focussing on the different members of that set, and their relationship to each other, each member can be understood better, as can the nature of the set itself. In striving for this, there are various methodological options available to us, which individually or collectively could progress our understanding of each disciplinary approach and the larger set to which they belong. This in turn could transform the definition, selection, combination and application of disciplinary approaches, both within disciplinary boundaries and also beyond them. To achieve this, a programme for future work would include several key points:

- *researchers* interested in a *single* disciplinary approach should
  - review work on other disciplinary approaches to identify similarities and differences, whether conceptual, methodological or pedagogical
  - specify the kinds of things that their disciplinary approach is, and ensure that any components are consistent with that
  - review work on taxonomies of thinking and higher-order thinking skills to build on them or contribute toward them

- *researchers* interested in *multiple* disciplinary approaches should (in addition to the above points)
  - design and conduct studies to understand how different disciplinary approaches arise and develop in individuals and groups
  - design and conduct studies to compare the disciplinary approaches exhibited in different sub-disciplines (within and across disciplines)
  - design and conduct studies to compare how individuals and groups from different disciplines approach the same task
  - explore alternative categorisations of disciplinary approaches (e.g. not necessarily referring to design or entrepreneurship)
  - develop and test maps of the relationships between disciplinary approaches

- *educators* interested in single or multiple disciplinary approaches should
  - communicate the general concept of disciplinary approaches to learners
  - situate any specific disciplinary approach in the context of other approaches that are already known to learners
  - explicitly deal with the concept of transfer, and explore the challenges of far transfer
  - design educational interventions in such a way that transfer can be measured and assessed.

To establish the kind of thing that disciplinary approaches are, I began this work with the stub of a joke about a designer, an ecologist and an entrepreneur. Reconsidering the assumptions behind that joke now, perhaps it is not so important how each individual thinks and behaves in isolation, but is more a matter of how their thoughts and behaviours relate to each other's. If they could identify and explore those relationships then they would be better placed to understand what distinguishes each of them, but also what unites them. They might even decide that other disciplinary approaches are required to address the scenarios they confront, and then identify people who see the world, orient toward it and act upon it in ways that complement their own. For them to do this, it would be useful to have access to a map showing many different approaches, and how those approaches are related. In this work, I have explored many of the problems that would be encountered in trying to piece together such a map, but I hope to have also illustrated some of the possible forms such a map could eventually take, the source material that would be required to construct it and the benefits it might subsequently offer.

References

Acar, O. A., Tarakci, M., & van Knippenberg, D. (2019). Creativity and Innovation Under Constraints: A Cross-Disciplinary Integrative Review. *Journal of Management, 45*(1), 96–121. https://doi.org/10.1177/01492063 18805832.

Aier, S., Labusch, N., & Pähler, P. (2015). Implementing Architectural Thinking. In A. Persson & J. Stirna (Eds.), *Advanced Information Systems Engineering Workshops* (pp. 389–400). Springer. https://doi.org/10.1007/978-3-319-19243-7_36.

Algani, Y. M. A., & Jmal, E. (2020). The Effectiveness of a Program for Developing the Skills of Mathematical Thinking for First Year Preparatory Pupils. *Journal of Gifted Education and Creativity, 7*(2), 41–51.

Ambole, A. (2020). Rethinking Design Making and Design Thinking in Africa. *Design and Culture, 12*(3), 331–350. https://doi.org/10.1080/17547075.2020.1788257.

Andrews, T., & Burke, F. (2007). *What Does It Mean to Think Historically? | Perspectives on History |* AHA. www.historians.org/publications-and-direc tories/perspectives-on-history/january-2007/what-does-it-mean-to-think-historically

Antle, A. N. (2017). Making Sense of Design Thinking. *She Ji: The Journal of Design, Economics, and Innovation, 3*(2), 92–96. https://doi.org/10.1016/j.sheji.2017.10.003.

Arnold, R. D., & Wade, J. P. (2015). A Definition of Systems Thinking: A Systems Approach. *Procedia Computer Science, 44*, 669–678. https://doi.org/10.1016/j.procs.2015.03.050.

Arthur, W. B. (2009). *The Nature of Technology: What It Is and How It Evolves.* Free Press.

Askeland, B. (2020). The Potential of Abductive Legal Reasoning. *Ratio Juris, 33*(1), 66–81. https://doi.org/10.1111/raju.12268.

Athreya, B. H., & Mouza, C. (2017). What Is Thinking? In B. H. Athreya & C. Mouza (Eds.), *Thinking Skills for the Digital Generation: The Development of Thinking and Learning in the Age of Information* (pp. 25–35). Springer. https://doi.org/10.1007/978-3-319-12364-6_3.

Auernhammer, J., & Roth, B. (2021). The Origin and Evolution of Stanford University's Design Thinking: From Product Design to Design Thinking in Innovation Management. *Journal of Product Innovation Management, 38*(6), 623–644. https://doi.org/10.1111/jpim.12594.

Barak, M., & Levenberg, A. (2016). A Model of Flexible Thinking in Contemporary Education. *Thinking Skills and Creativity*, *22*, 74–85. https://doi.org/10.1016/j.tsc.2016.09.003.

Barnett, S. M., & Ceci, S. J. (2002). When and Where Do We Apply What We Learn? A Taxonomy for Far Transfer. *Psychological Bulletin*, *128*(4), 612–637. https://doi.org/10.1037/0033-2909.128.4.612.

Barr, V., & Stephenson, C. (2011). Bringing Computational Thinking to K-12: What is Involved and What is the Role of the Computer Science Education Community? *ACM Inroads*, *2*(1), 48–54. https://doi.org/10.1145/1929887.1929905.

Bashford, T., Myint, P. P. N., Win, S. et al., (2018). A Systems Approach to Traumacare in Myanmar: From Health Partnership to Academic Collaboration. *Future Healthcare Journal*, *5*(3), 171–175. https://doi.org/10.7861/futurehosp.5-3-171.

Becher, T. (ed.). (2017). *Professional Practices: Commitment & Capability in a Changing Environment*. Routledge. https://doi.org/10.4324/97813512 89689.

Binah-Pollak, A., Hazzan, O., Mike, K., & Hacohen, R. L. (2024). Anthropological Thinking in Data Science Education: Thinking within Context. *Education and Information Technologies*. https://doi.org/10.1007/s10639-023-12444-7.

Blackwell, A., Church, L., & Green, T. (2008). The Abstract is 'an Enemy': Alternative Perspectives to Computational Thinking. *In Proceedings PPIG'08, 20th Annual Workshop of the Psychology of Programming Interest Group*, *1*, 34–43.

Blackwell, A., Wilson, L., Boulton, C., & Knell, J. (2010). *Creating Value across Boundaries: Maximising the Return from Interdisciplinary Innovation* (p. 31). Nesta. https://media.nesta.org.uk/documents/creating_value_across_boundaries.pdf.

Boland, R., & Collopy, F. (Eds.). (2004). *Managing as Designing*. Stanford Business Books.

Breslin, D. (2016). What Evolves in Organizational Co-Evolution? *Journal of Management & Governance*, *20*(1), 45–67. https://doi.org/10.1007/s10997-014-9302-0.

Brooks, C., Butt, G., & Fargher, M. (Eds.). (2017). *The Power of Geographical Thinking*. Springer. https://doi.org/10.1007/978-3-319-49986-4.

Brown, T. (2008, June 1). Design Thinking. *Harvard Business Review*, 1–9. https://hbr.org/2008/06/design-thinking.

Buchanan, R. (2019). Systems Thinking and Design Thinking: The Search for Principles in the World We Are Making. *She Ji: The Journal of Design,*

Economics, and Innovation, *5*(2), 85–104. https://doi.org/10.1016/j.sheji .2019.04.001.

Bunderson, J. S., & Sutcliffe, K. M. (2002). Comparing Alternative Conceptualizations of Functional Diversity in Management Teams: Process and Performance Effects. *Academy of Management Journal*, *45*(5), 875–893. https://doi.org/10.5465/3069319.

Burton, L. (1984). Mathematical Thinking: The Struggle for Meaning. *Journal for Research in Mathematics Education*, *15*(1), 35–49. https://doi.org/ 10.5951/jresematheduc.15.1.0035.

Camelia, F., & Ferris, T. L. J. (2016). Systems Thinking in Systems Engineering. *INCOSE International Symposium*, *26*(1), 1657–1674. https:// doi.org/10.1002/j.2334-5837.2016.00252.x.

Cao, L. (2018). *Data Science Thinking: The Next Scientific, Technological and Economic Revolution*. Springer. https://cam.ldls.org.uk/vdc_10006955 5981.0x000001.

Capra, F., & Luisi, P. L. (2014). *The Systems View of Life: A Unifying Vision*. Cambridge University Press. https://doi.org/10.1017/CBO9780511895555.

Carlgren, L., Elmquist, M., & Rauth, I. (2016). The Challenges of Using Design Thinking in Industry – Experiences from Five Large Firms. *Creativity and Innovation Management*, *25*(3), 344–362. https://doi.org/10.1111/caim .12176.

Carlgren, L., Rauth, I., & Elmquist, M. (2016). Framing Design Thinking: The Concept in Idea and Enactment. *Creativity and Innovation Management*, *25* (1), 38–57. https://doi.org/10.1111/caim.12153.

Cavaleri, S., & Sterman, J. D. (1997). Towards Evaluation of Systems-Thinking Interventions: A Case Study. *System Dynamics Review*, *13*(2), 171–186. https://doi.org/10.1002/(SICI)1099-1727(199722)13:2<171::AID-SDR123>3.0.CO;2-9.

Chance, B. L. (2002). Components of Statistical Thinking and Implications for Instruction and Assessment. *Journal of Statistics Education*, *10*(3), 1–14. https://doi.org/10.1080/10691898.2002.11910677.

Chandler, J. (2009). Introduction: Doctrines, Disciplines, Discourses, Departments. *Critical Inquiry*, *35*(4), 729–746. https://doi.org/10.1086/ 599585.

Chen, C.-C., & Crilly, N. (2016). Describing Complex Design Practices with a Cross-Domain Framework: Learning from Synthetic Biology and Swarm Robotics. *Research in Engineering Design*, *27*(3), 291–305. https://doi.org/ 10.1007/s00163-016-0219-2.

Christensen, B. T., Arendt, K. M., McElheron, P., & Ball, L. J. (2023). The Design Entrepreneur: How Adaptive Cognition and Formal Design Training

Create Entrepreneurial Self-efficacy and Entrepreneurial Intention. *Design Studies*, *86*, 1–23. https://doi.org/10.1016/j.destud.2023.101181.

Clarke, L. (2008). Possibilistic Thinking: A New Conceptual Tool for Thinking about Extreme Events. *Social Research*, *75*(3), 669–690.

Coelen, J., & Smulders, F. E. H. M. (2023). Educating Entrepreneurship through Design. In J. H. Block, J. Halberstadt, N. Högsdal, A. Kuckertz, & H. Neergaard (Eds.), *Progress in Entrepreneurship Education and Training: New Methods, Tools, and Lessons Learned from Practice* (pp. 401–415). Springer. https://doi.org/10.1007/978-3-031-28559-2_26.

Cole, M., & Means, B. (1981). *Comparative Studies of how People Think: An Introduction*. Harvard University Press.

Collins, H. (2018). Studies of Expertise and Experience. *Topoi*, *37*(1), 67–77. https://doi.org/10.1007/s11245-016-9412-1.

Collopy, F. (2019). Why the Failure of Systems Thinking Should Inform the Future of Design Thinking (06.07.09). *Design Issues*, *35*(2), 97–100. https://doi.org/10.1162/desi_a_00538.

Costa, A. L., & Kallick, B. (2008). *Learning and Leading with Habits of Mind: 16 Essential Characteristics for Success*. Association for Supervision & Curriculum Development.

Craft, A. (2015). Possibility Thinking. In R. Wegerif, L. Li, & J. C. Kaufman (eds.), *The Routledge International Handbook of Research on Teaching Thinking* (pp. 153–167). Routledge.

Crilly, N. (2010). The Structure of Design Revolutions: Kuhnian Paradigm Shifts in Creative Problem Solving. *Design Issues*, *26*(1), 54–66. https://doi.org/10.1162/desi.2010.26.1.54.

Crilly, N. (2021a). The Evolution of "Co-evolution" (Part I): Problem Solving, Problem Finding, and Their Interaction in Design and Other Creative Practices. *She Ji: The Journal of Design, Economics, and Innovation*, *7*(3), 309–332. https://doi.org/10.1016/j.sheji.2021.07.003.

Crilly, N. (2021b). The Evolution of 'Co-evolution' (Part II): The Biological Analogy, Different Kinds of Co-evolution, and Proposals for Conceptual Expansion. *She Ji: The Journal of Design, Economics, and Innovation*, *7*(3), 333–355. https://doi.org/10.1016/j.sheji.2021.07.004.

Crilly, N., Blackwell, A. F., & Clarkson, P. J. (2006). Graphic Elicitation: Using Research Diagrams as Interview Stimuli. *Qualitative Research*, *6*(3), 341–366. https://doi.org/10.1177/1468794106065007.

Crombie, A. C. (1988). Designed in the Mind: Western Visions of Science, Nature and Humankind. *History of Science*, *26*(1), 1–12. https://doi.org/10.1177/007327538802600101.

Cronin, M. A., & George, E. (2023). The Why and How of the Integrative Review. *Organizational Research Methods, 26*(1), 168–192. https://doi.org/10.1177/1094428120935507.

Cross, N. (1982). Designerly Ways of Knowing. *Design Studies, 3*(4), 221–227. https://doi.org/10.1016/0142-694X(82)90040-0.

Cross, N. (2023). Design Thinking: What Just Happened? *Design Studies, 86*, 101187. https://doi.org/10.1016/j.destud.2023.101187.

Crudo, B. (2020, April 30). *How to Embrace 'Entrepreneurial Thinking' Even If You're Not an Entrepreneur.* Fast Company. www.fastcompany.com/90498511/how-to-embrace-entrepreneurial-thinking-even-if-youre-not-an-entrepreneur.

Cuoco, A., Goldenberg, P. E., & Mark, J. (1996). Habits of Mind: An Organizing Principle for Mathematics Curricula. *The Journal of Mathematical Behavior, 15*(4), 375–402. https://doi.org/10.1016/S0732-3123(96)90023-1.

Daspit, J. J., Fox, C. J., & Findley, S. K. (2023). Entrepreneurial Mindset: An Integrated Definition, a Review of Current Insights, and Directions for Future Research. *Journal of Small Business Management, 61*(1), 1–33. https://doi.org/10.1080/00472778.2021.1907583.

de Savigny, D., & Taghreed, A. (eds.). (2009). *Systems Thinking for Health Systems Strengthening.* World Health Organization. http://rgdoi.net/10.13140/RG.2.1.4720.4325.

Denning, P. J. (2013). Design Thinking. *Communications of the ACM, 56*(12), 29–31. https://doi.org/10.1145/2535915.

Denning, P. J., & Tedre, M. (2019). *Computational Thinking.* MIT Press.

Denning, P. J., & Tedre, M. (2021). Computational Thinking for Professionals. *Communications of the ACM, 64*(12), 30–33. https://doi.org/10.1145/3491268.

Donald, J. G. (2002). *Learning To Think: Disciplinary Perspectives. The Jossey-Bass Higher and Adult Education Series.* Jossey-Bass.

Dorst, K. (2011). The Core of 'Design Thinking' and its Application. *Design Studies, 32*(6), 521–532. https://doi.org/10.1016/j.destud.2011.07.006.

Dunbar, K., & Fugelsang, J. (2005). Scientific Thinking and Reasoning. In K. J. Holyoak & R. G. Morrison (Eds.), *The Cambridge Handbook of Thinking and Reasoning* (pp. 705–725). Cambridge University Press.

Dunne, D., & Martin, R. (2006). Design Thinking and How It Will Change Management Education: An Interview and Discussion. *Academy of Management Learning & Education, 5*(4), 512–523. https://doi.org/10.5465/amle.2006.23473212.

Dzombak, R., & Beckman, S. (2020). Unpacking Capabilities Underlying Design (thinking) Process. *International Journal of Engineering Education, 36*(2), 574–585.

Easterbrook, S. (2014). From Computational Thinking to Systems Thinking: A Conceptual toolkit for Sustainability Computing. *ICT for Sustainability 2014 (ICT4S-14)*, 235–244. https://doi.org/10.2991/ict4s-14.2014.28.

Eckert, C., Blackwell, A., Stacey, M., Earl, C., & Church, L. (2012). Sketching across Design Domains: Roles and Formalities. *Artificial Intelligence for Engineering Design, Analysis and Manufacturing, 26*(3), 245–266. https://doi.org/10.1017/S0890060412000133.

Endy, D. (2005). Foundations for Engineering Biology. *Nature, 438*(7067), 449–453. https://doi.org/10.1038/nature04342.

Engelke, M. (2019). *How to Think Like an Anthropologist*. Princeton University Press.

English, L. (2023). Ways of Thinking in STEM-based Problem Solving. *ZDM: The International Journal on Mathematics Education, 55*, 1219–1230 . https://doi.org/10.1007/s11858-023-01474-7.

Ennis, R. H. (1964). A Definition of Critical Thinking. *The Reading Teacher, 17*(8), 599–612.

Ennis, R. H. (1989). Critical Thinking and Subject Specificity: Clarification and Needed Research. *Educational Researcher, 18*(3), 4–10. https://doi.org/10.3102/0013189X018003004.

Evans, J. St. B. T., & Over, D. E. (2013). Reasoning to and from Belief: Deduction and Induction are still Distinct. *Thinking & Reasoning, 19*(3–4), 267–283. https://doi.org/10.1080/13546783.2012.745450.

Farrell, R., & Hooker, C. (2013). Design, Science and Wicked Problems. *Design Studies, 34*(6), 681–705. https://doi.org/10.1016/j.destud.2013.05.001.

Fischer, J. (2016). Managing Research Environments: Heterarchies in Academia. A Response to Cumming. *Trends in Ecology & Evolution, 31*(12), 900–902. https://doi.org/10.1016/j.tree.2016.09.010.

Flanagan, D. P., & Dixon, S. G. (2014). The Cattell-Horn-Carroll Theory of Cognitive Abilities. In C. R. Reynolds, K. J. Vannest, and E. Fletcher-Janzen (Eds.), *Encyclopedia of Special Education*. John Wiley & Sons. https://doi.org/10.1002/9781118660584.ese0431.

Ford, D. N., & Sterman, J. D. (1998). Expert Knowledge Elicitation to Improve Formal and Mental Models. *System Dynamics Review, 14*(4), 309–340.

Frascari, M. (2009). Lines as Architectural Thinking. *Architectural Theory Review, 14*(3), 200–212. https://doi.org/10.1080/13264820903341605.

Frederiksen, D. L., & Brem, A. (2017). How Do Entrepreneurs Think They Create Value? A Scientific Reflection of Eric Ries' Lean Startup approach. *International Entrepreneurship and Management Journal, 13*(1), 169–189. https://doi.org/10.1007/s11365-016-0411-x.

Galle, P., & Kroes, P. (2014). Science and Design: Identical Twins? *Design Studies*, *35*(3), 201–231. https://doi.org/10.1016/j.destud.2013.12.002.

Garbuio, M., Dong, A., Lin, N., Tschang, T., & Lovallo, D. (2018). Demystifying the Genius of Entrepreneurship: How Design Cognition Can Help Create the Next Generation of Entrepreneurs. *Academy of Management Learning & Education*, *17*(1), 41–61. https://doi.org/10.5465/amle.2016.0040.

Gardner, P. L. (1975). Attitudes to Science: A Review. *Studies in Science Education*, *2*(1), 1–41. https://doi.org/10.1080/03057267508559818.

Gauld, C. F., & Hukins, A. A. (1980). Scientific Attitudes: A Review. *Studies in Science Education*, *7*(1), 129–161. https://doi.org/10.1080/03057268008559877.

Gentner, D., & Maravilla, F. (2018). Analogical Reasoning. In L. J. Ball & V. A. Thompson (Eds.), *International Handbook of Thinking and Reasoning* (pp. 186–203). Routledge & CRC Press.

Geva-May, I. (2005). Thinking Like a Policy Analyst. In I. Geva-May (ed.), *Thinking Like a Policy Analyst: Policy Analysis as a Clinical Profession* (pp. 15–50). Palgrave Macmillan US. https://doi.org/10.1057/9781403980939_2.

Gharajedaghi, J. (2011). *Systems Thinking: Managing Chaos and Complexity: A Platform for Designing Business Architecture*. Elsevier.

Gibbs, K. D., Han, A., & Lun, J. (2019). Demographic Diversity in Teams: The Challenges, Benefits, and Management Strategies. In K. L. Hall, A. L. Vogel, & R. T. Croyle (Eds.), *Strategies for Team Science Success: Handbook of Evidence-Based Principles for Cross-Disciplinary Science and Practical Lessons Learned from Health Researchers* (pp. 197–205). Springer. https://doi.org/10.1007/978-3-030-20992-6_15.

Gieryn, T. F. (1983). Boundary-Work and the Demarcation of Science from Non-Science: Strains and Interests in Professional Ideologies of Scientists. *American Sociological Review*, *48*(6), 781–795. https://doi.org/10.2307/2095325.

Glen, R., Suciu, C., & Baughn, C. (2014). The Need for Design Thinking in Business Schools. *Academy of Management Learning & Education*, *13*(4), 653–667.

Goodchild, M. (2021). Relational Systems Thinking: That's How Change is Going to Come, From Our Earth Mother. *Journal of Awareness-Based Systems Change*, *1*(1), 75–103. https://doi.org/10.47061/jabsc.v1i1.577.

Goodyear, P., & Markauskaite, L. (2017). *Epistemic Fluency and Professional Education: Innovation, Knowledgeable Action and Working Knowledge*. Springer. https://cam.ldls.org.uk/vdc_100068972000.0x000001.

Gorman, M. E. (2006). Scientific and Technological Thinking. *Review of General Psychology*, *10*(2), 113–129. https://doi.org/10.1037/1089-2680 .10.2.113.

Gornall, S., Chambers, M. R., & Claxton, G. (2005). *Building Learning Power in Action*. TLO .

Gould, R. (2021). Toward Data-Scientific Thinking. *Teaching Statistics*, *43*(S1), S11–S22. https://doi.org/10.1111/test.12267.

Greenwood, R., Suddaby, R., & Hinings, C. R. (2002). Theorizing Change: The Role of Professional Associations in the Transformation of Institutionalized Fields. *Academy of Management Journal*, *45*(1), 58–80. https://doi.org/ 10.5465/3069285.

Grégoire, D. A., Corbett, A. C., & McMullen, J. S. (2011). The Cognitive Perspective in Entrepreneurship: An Agenda for Future Research. *Journal of Management Studies*, *48*(6), 1443–1477. https://doi.org/10.1111/j.1467-6486.2010.00922.x.

Griffiths, D. (1997). The Case for Theoretical Pluralism. *Educational Management & Administration*, *25*(4), 371–380. https://doi.org/10.1177/ 0263211X97254003.

Grimes, M. G., & Vogus, T. J. (2021). Inconceivable! Possibilistic Thinking and the Sociocognitive Underpinnings of Entrepreneurial Responses to Grand Challenges. *Organization Theory*, *2*(2), 1–11. https://doi.org/10.1177/ 26317877211005780.

Groth, C. (2016). Design- and Craft Thinking Analysed as Embodied Cognition. *Form Akademisk*, *9*(1), Article 1. https://doi.org/10.7577/ formakademisk.1481.

Hacking, I. (1994). Styles of Scientific Thinking or Reasoning: A New Analytical Tool for Historians and Philosophers of the Sciences. In K. Gavroglu, J. Christianidis, & E. Nicolaidis (Eds.), *Trends in the Historiography of Science* (Vol. 151, pp. 31–48). Springer Netherlands. https://doi.org/10.1007/978-94-017-3596-4.

Halpern, D. F., & Sternberg, R. J. (2020). An Introduction to Critical Thinking: Maybe It Will Change Your Life. In R. J. Sternberg & D. F. Halpern (eds.), *Critical Thinking in Psychology* (2nd ed., pp. 1–9). Cambridge University Press. https://doi.org/10.1017/9781108684354.002.

Hassi, L., & Laakso, M. (2011). Design Thinking in the Management Discourse: Defining the Elements of the Concept. *18th International Product Development Management Conference, Innovate Through Design*. https://research.aalto.fi/en/publications/design-thinking-in-the-manage ment-discourse-defining-the-elements.

Hay, L., Cash, P., & McKilligan, S. (2020). The Future of Design Cognition Analysis. *Design Science*, *6*, 1–26. https://doi.org/10.1017/dsj.2020.20.

Haynie, J. M., Shepherd, D., Mosakowski, E., & Earley, P. C. (2010). A Situated Metacognitive Model of the Entrepreneurial Mindset. *Journal of Business Venturing*, *25*(2), 217–229. https://doi.org/10.1016/j.jbusvent.2008.10.001.

Heylighen, A., & Dong, A. (2019). To Empathise or not to Empathise? Empathy and its Limits in Design. *Design Studies*, *65*, 107–124. https://doi.org/10.1016/j.destud.2019.10.007.

Heyne, P. T., Boettke, P. J., & Prychitko, D. L. (2013). *The Economic Way of Thinking* (13th ed.). Pearson. https://cam.ldls.org.uk/vdc_100048053355.0x000001.

Higgins, M. (2020, November 5). *Council Post: The Benefits of Incorporating Design Thinking Into Business*. Forbes. www.forbes.com/sites/forbestech council/2020/11/05/the-benefits-of-incorporating-design-thinking-into-busi ness/.

Hitchcock, D. (2020). Critical Thinking. In E. N. Zalta (Ed.), *The Stanford Encyclopedia of Philosophy*. Metaphysics Research Lab, Stanford University. https://plato.stanford.edu/archives/fall2020/entries/critical-thinking/.

Hoberman, B. (2015, March 3). *Business Starts at School in This Golden Age for Young Founders*. Financial Times. www.ft.com/content/1f050bd6-c0d0-11e4-876d-00144feab7de.

Hua, M., Harvey, S., & Rietzschel, E.F. (2022). Unpacking 'Ideas' in Creative Work: A Multidisciplinary Review. *Academy of Management Annals*, *16*(2), 621–656. https://doi.org/10.5465/annals.2020.0210.

Illari, P., Russo, F., Williamson, J., & Lagnado, D. (2011). Causal Thinking. In P. M. Illari, F. Russo, J. Williamson (Eds.), *Causality in the Sciences* (pp. 129–149). Oxford University Press.

Ings, W. (2015). Malleable Thought: The Role of Craft Thinking in Practice-Led Graphic Design. *International Journal of Art & Design Education*, *34*(2), 180–191. https://doi.org/10.1111/jade.12013.

Inns, T., & Mountain, R. (2020). Designing 'Realistic' Healthcare Improvement. *Design Management Review*, *31*, 12–19. https://doi.org/10.1111/drev.12206.

Ireland, R. D., & Webb, J. W. (2007). A Cross-Disciplinary Exploration of Entrepreneurship Research. *Journal of Management*, *33*(6), 891–927. https://doi.org/10.1177/0149206307307643.

Jackson, M. C. (2003). *Systems Thinking: Creative Holism for Managers*. Wiley.

Jackson, P. (2006). Thinking Geographically. *Geography*, *91*(3), 199–204. https://doi.org/10.1080/00167487.2006.12094167.

Jacob, M., Lundqvist, M., & Hellsmark, H. (2003). Entrepreneurial Transformations in the Swedish University System: The Case of Chalmers University of Technology. *Research Policy, 32*(9), 1555–1568. https://doi.org/10.1016/S0048-7333(03)00024-6.

Johansson-Sköldberg, U., Woodilla, J., & Çetinkaya, M. (2013). Design Thinking: Past, Present and Possible Futures. *Creativity and Innovation Management, 22*(2), 121–146. https://doi.org/10.1111/caim.12023.

Jones, A., Buntting, C., Hipkins, R. et al. (2012). Developing Students' Futures Thinking in Science Education. *Research in Science Education, 42*(4), 687–708. https://doi.org/10.1007/s11165-011-9214-9.

Jones, W. A. (2011). Variation among Academic Disciplines: An Update on Analytical Frameworks and Research. *The Journal of the Professoriate, 6*(1), 9–27.

Karkdijk, J., van der Schee, J., & Admiraal, W. (2013). Effects of Teaching with Mysteries on Students' Geographical Thinking Skills. *International Research in Geographical and Environmental Education, 22*(3), 183–190. https://doi.org/10.1080/10382046.2013.817664.

Kaur, M., & Craven, L. (2020). Systems Thinking: Practical Insights on Systems-Led Design in Socio-Technical Engineering Systems. In A. Maier, J. Oehmen, & P. E. Vermaas (Eds.), *Handbook of Engineering Systems Design* (pp. 189–217). Springer International Publishing. https://doi.org/10.1007/978-3-030-46054-9_36-3.

Kavanagh, S. (2021). *Entrepreneurial Thinking in Local Government.* City of Lancaster, California. www.gfoa.org/materials/entrepreneurial-thinking-in-local-government.

Keleşzade, G., Güneyli, A., & Özkul, A. E. (2018). Effectiveness of History Teaching Based on Social Constructivist Learning and Development of Historical Thinking Skills. *TED EĞİTİM VE BİLİM, 43*(195), 167–191. https://doi.org/10.15390/EB.2018.7479.

Kelly, N., & Gero, J. S. (2021). Design Thinking and Computational Thinking: A Dual Process Model for Addressing Design Problems. *Design Science, 7*, e8. https://doi.org/10.1017/dsj.2021.7.

Kimbell, L. (2011). Rethinking Design Thinking: Part I. *Design and Culture, 3* (3), 285–306. https://doi.org/10.2752/175470811X13071166525216.

Klenner, N. F., Gemser, G., & Karpen, I. O. (2022). Entrepreneurial Ways of Designing and Designerly Ways of Entrepreneuring: Exploring the Relationship between Design Thinking and Effectuation Theory. *Journal of Product Innovation Management, 39*(1), 66–94. https://doi.org/10.1111/jpim.12587.

Knight, T. F. (2005). Engineering Novel Life. *Molecular Systems Biology*, *1*(1), 1. https://doi.org/10.1038/msb4100028.

Kolko, J. (2018). The Divisiveness of Design Thinking. *Interactions*, *25*(3), 28–34. https://doi.org/10.1145/3194313.

Kong, S.-C. (2019). Components and Methods of Evaluating Computational Thinking for Fostering Creative Problem-Solvers in Senior Primary School Education. In S.-C. Kong & H. Abelson (Eds.), *Computational Thinking Education* (pp. 119–141). Springer Singapore. https://doi.org/10.1007/978-981-13-6528-7.

Krishnan, A. (2009). *What are Academic Disciplines? Some Observations on the Disciplinarity vs. Interdisciplinarity Debate* (ESRC National Centre for Research Methods (NCRM) Working Paper Series). https://eprints.ncrm.ac.uk/id/eprint/783/.

Krueger, N. F. (2007). What Lies Beneath? The Experiential Essence of Entrepreneurial Thinking. *Entrepreneurship Theory and Practice*, *31*(1), 123–138. https://doi.org/10.1111/j.1540-6520.2007.00166.x.

Kurtmollaiev, S., Pedersen, P. E., Fjuk, A., & Kvale, K. (2018). Developing Managerial Dynamic Capabilities: A Quasi-Experimental Field Study of the Effects of Design Thinking Training. *Academy of Management Learning & Education*, *17*(2), 184–202. https://doi.org/10.5465/amle.2016.0187.

Langer, J. A. (1998). Thinking and Doing Literature: An Eight-Year Study. *The English Journal*, *87*(2), 16. https://doi.org/10.2307/821546.

Langer, J. A., Confer, C., & Sawyer, M. (1993). *Teaching Disciplinary Thinking in Academic Coursework* (2.19, p. 46). National Research Centre on Literature Teaching and Learning.

Lavrsen, J. C., Daalhuizen, J., & Carbon, C.-C. (2023). The Design Mindset Inventory (D-Mindset0): A Preliminary Instrument For Measuring Design Mindset. *Proceedings of ICED23*, *3*, 3355–3364. https://doi.org/10.1017/pds.2023.336.

Lewens, T. (2009) What Is Wrong with Typological Thinking?. *Philosophy of Science*, *76*(3), 355–371. https://doi.org/10.1086/649810.

Lewens, T. (2015). *Cultural Evolution: Conceptual Challenges*. Oxford University Press.

Lewrick, M., Link, P., & Leifer, L. (2018). *The Design Thinking Playbook: Mindful Digital Transformation of Teams, Products, Services, Businesses and Ecosystems*. John Wiley & Sons.

Liedtka, J., King, A., & Bennett, K. (2013). *Solving Problems with Design Thinking: Ten Stories of What Works*. Columbia University Press.

Liedtka, J., & Ogilvie, T. (2011). *Designing for Growth: A Design Thinking Tool Kit for Managers*. Columbia University Press.

Liedtka, J., Sheikh, A., Gilmer, C., Kupetz, M., & Wilcox, L. (2020). The Use of Design Thinking in the U.S. Federal Government. *Public Performance & Management Review*, *43*(1), 157–179. https://doi.org/10.1080/15309576.2019.1657916.

Lilienfeld, S. O., Basterfield, C., Bowes, S. M., & Costello, T. H. (2020). Nobelists Gone Wild: Case Studies in the Domain Specificity of Critical Thinking. In D. F. Halpern & R. J. Sternberg (Eds.), *Critical Thinking in Psychology* (2nd ed., pp. 10–38). Cambridge University Press. https://doi.org/10.1017/9781108684354.003.

Litster, G., Hurst, A., & Cardoso, C. (2023). A Systems Thinking Inspired Approach to Understanding Design Activity. In J. S. Gero (Ed.), *Design Computing and Cognition DCC'22* (pp. 161–177). Cham: Springer.

Loftus, S. (2018). Thinking Like a Scientist and Thinking Like a Doctor. *Medical Science Educator*, *28*(1), 251–254. https://doi.org/10.1007/s40670-017-0498-x.

Lucas, B., Hanson, J., & Claxton, G. (2014). *Thinking Like an Engineer: Implications for the Education System: (A Report for the Royal Academy of Engineering Standing Committee for Education and Training)*. Royal Academy of Engineering (United Kingdom).

Madson, M. J. (2021). Making Sense of Design Thinking: A Primer for Medical Teachers. *Medical Teacher*, *43*(10), 1115–1121. https://doi.org/10.1080/0142159X.2021.1874327.

Mamakani, K., & Ruskey, F. (2012). *A New Rose: The First Simple Symmetric 11-Venn Diagram* (arXiv:1207.6452). arXiv. http://arxiv.org/abs/1207.6452.

Mankiw, N. G., & Taylor, M. P. (2014). *Economics* (3rd ed.). Cengage Learning EMEA. http://cws.cengage.co.uk/mankiw_taylor2/.

McComb, C., & Jablokow, K. (2022). A Conceptual Framework for Multidisciplinary Design Research with Example Application to Agent-Based Modeling. *Design Studies*, *78*, 101074. https://doi.org/10.1016/j.destud.2021.101074.

McCool, S. F., Freimund, W. A., Breen, C. et al. (2015). Benefiting from complexity thinking. In G. L. Worboys, M. Lockwood, A. Kothari, S. Feary, & I. Pulsford (Eds.), *Protected Area Governance and Management* (pp. 291–326). ANU Press. https://www.jstor.org/stable/j.ctt1657v5d.17.

McGrath, R. G., & MacMillan, I. C. (2000). *The Entrepreneurial Mindset: Strategies for Continuously Creating Opportunity in an Age of Uncertainty*. Harvard Business Press.

McKim, R. H. (1980). *Experiences in Visual Thinking*. PWS.

McPeck, J. E. (1981). *Critical Thinking and Education*. St. Martin's Press.

McPeck, J. E. (1990). Critical Thinking and Subject Specificity: A Reply to Ennis. *Educational Researcher, 19*(4), 10–12.

Meadows, D. H. (2008). *Thinking in Systems: A Primer*. Chelsea Green.

Mello, A. L., & Rentsch, J. R. (2015). Cognitive Diversity in Teams: A Multidisciplinary Review. *Small Group Research, 46*(6), 623–658. https://doi.org/10.1177/1046496415602558.

Messer-Davidow, E., Shumway, D. R., & Sylvan, D. (1993). *Knowledges: Historical and Critical Studies in Disciplinarity*. University of Virginia Press.

Micheli, P., Wilner, S. J. S., Bhatti, S. H., Mura, M., & Beverland, M. B. (2019). Doing Design Thinking: Conceptual Review, Synthesis, and Research Agenda. *Journal of Product Innovation Management, 36*(2), 124–148. https://doi.org/10.1111/jpim.12466.

Milani, A., & Farinella, P. (1994). The Age of the Veritas Asteroid Family Deduced by Chaotic Chronology. *Nature, 370*(6484), Article 6484. https://doi.org/10.1038/370040a0.

Momsen, J., Speth, E. B., Wyse, S., & Long, T. (2022). Using Systems and Systems Thinking to Unify Biology Education. *CBE Life Sciences Education, 21*(2), es3. https://doi.org/10.1187/cbe.21-05-0118.

Moore, T. J. (2011). Critical Thinking and Disciplinary Thinking: A Continuing Debate. *Higher Education Research & Development, 30*(3), 261–274. https://doi.org/10.1080/07294360.2010.501328.

Nesvorný, D., Bottke, W. F., Vokrouhlický, D., Morbidelli, A., & Jedicke, R. (2005). Asteroid Families. *Proceedings of the International Astronomical Union, 1*(S229), 289–299. https://doi.org/10.1017/S1743921305006800.

Newton, D. (2005). The Nature of Thinking and Thinking Skills. In D. Moseley, D. P. Newton, J. Miller et al. (Eds.), *Frameworks for Thinking: A Handbook for Teaching and Learning* (pp. 8–32). Cambridge University Press. https://doi.org/10.1017/CBO9780511489914.004.

Noll, V. H. (1935). Measuring the Scientific Attitude. *The Journal of Abnormal and Social Psychology, 30*(2), 145–154. https://doi.org/10.1037/h0059829.

Novick, L. R., & Catley, K. M. (2016). Fostering 21st-Century Evolutionary Reasoning: Teaching Tree Thinking to Introductory Biology Students. *CBE—Life Sciences Education, 15*(4), ar66. https://doi.org/10.1187/cbe.15-06-0127.

Nussbaum, B. (2004). The Power of Design: A Tiny Firm Called IDEO Redefined Good Design by Creating Experiences, Not Just Products. Now It's Changing the Way Companies Innovate. (Cover Story). *Business Week*, 1–9.

O'Hara, R. J. (1997). Population Thinking and Tree Thinking in Systematics. *Zoologica Scripta, 26*(4), 323–329. https://doi.org/10.1111/j.1463-6409.1997.tb00422.x.

Patel, S., & Mehta, K. (2017). Systems, Design, and Entrepreneurial Thinking: Comparative Frameworks. *Systemic Practice and Action Research, 30*(5), 515–533. https://doi.org/10.1007/s11213-016-9404-5.

Patel, V. L., Arocha, J. F., & Zhang, J. (2005). Thinking and Reasoning in Medicine. In K. J. Holyoak & R. G. Morrison (Eds.), *The Cambridge Handbook of Thinking and Reasoning* (pp. 727–750). Cambridge University Press.

Perkins, D. N. (1997). Epistemic Games. *International Journal of Educational Research, 27*(1), 49–61. https://doi.org/10.1016/S0883-0355 (97)88443-1.

Perkins, D. N., & Salomon, G. (1989). Are Cognitive Skills Context-Bound? *Educational Researcher, 18*(1), 16–25. https://doi.org/10.3102/00131 89X018001016.

Peschl, H., Deng, C., & Larson, N. (2021). Entrepreneurial Thinking: A Signature Pedagogy for an Uncertain 21st Century. *The International Journal of Management Education, 19*(1), 100427. https://doi.org/10.1016/ j.ijme.2020.100427.

Pourdehnad, J., Wilson, D., & Wexler, E. (2011, September 23). Systems & Design Thinking: A Conceptual Framework for Their Integration. *Proceedings of the 55th Annual Meeting of the ISSS, 55*(1), 1–15. https:// journals.isss.org/index.php/proceedings55th/article/view/1650.

Praslova, L. N. (2023, January 10). Today's Most Critical Workplace Challenges Are about Systems. *Harvard Business Review, 55*(1), 1–15. https://hbr.org/2023/01/todays-most-critical-workplace-challenges-are-about-systems.

Pressman, A. (2018). *Design Thinking: A Guide To Creative Problem Solving For Everyone.* Routledge. https://doi.org/10.4324/9781315561936.

Rapoport, N. B. (2002). Is Thinking Like a Lawyer Really What We Want to Teach? *Journal of the Association of Legal Writing Directors, 1*, 91–108.

Razzouk, R., & Shute, V. (2012). What Is Design Thinking and Why Is It Important? *Review of Educational Research, 82*(3), 330–348. https://doi .org/10.3102/0034654312457429.

Richardson, K. A. (2008). Managing Complex Organizations: Complexity Thinking and the Science and Art of Management. *Emergence: Complexity & Organization, 10*(2), 15.

Richmond, B. (1993). Systems Thinking: Critical Thinking Skills for the 1990s and Beyond. *System Dynamics Review, 9*(2), 113–133. https://doi.org/ 10.1002/sdr.4260090203.

Richmond, B. (2016, February 27). *The 'Thinking' in Systems Thinking: How Can We Make It Easier to Master?* The Systems Thinker. https://thesys

temsthinker.com/the-thinking-in-systems-thinking-how-can-we-make-it-eas
ier-to-master/.

Riess, W., & Mischo, C. (2010). Promoting Systems Thinking through Biology
Lessons. *International Journal of Science Education, 32*(6), 705–725. https://
doi.org/10.1080/09500690902769946.

Rodgers, C. (2002). Defining Reflection: Another Look at John Dewey and
Reflective Thinking. *Teachers College Record, 104*(4), 842–866. https://doi
.org/10.1111/1467-9620.00181.

Roehling, M. V., Cavanaugh, M. A., Moynihan, L. M., & Boswell, W. R.
(2000). The Nature of the New Employment Relationship: A Content
Analysis of the Practitioner and Academic Literatures. *Human Resource
Management, 39*(4), 305–320. https://doi.org/10.1002/1099-050X(200024)
39:4<305::AID-HRM3>3.0.CO;2-V.

Rosch, E. H. (1973). Natural Categories. *Cognitive Psychology, 4*(3), 328–350.
https://doi.org/10.1016/0010-0285(73)90017-0.

Rosvall, M., & Bergstrom, C. T. (2011). Multilevel Compression of Random
Walks on Networks Reveals Hierarchical Organization in Large Integrated
Systems. *PLOS ONE, 6*(4), e18209. https://doi.org/10.1371/journal.pone
.0018209.

Ruggiero, V. R. (1996). *A Guide to Sociological Thinking*. SAGE.

Rycroft-Smith, L., & Connolly, C. (2019). *Talking Point: What Are
Mathematical Thinking and Computational Thinking and What Is the
Relationship between Them?* (Espresso 24). Cambridge Mathematics.
www.cambridgemaths.org/Images/espresso_24_mathematical_and_compu
tational_thinking.pdf.

Sarasvathy, S. D. (2001). Causation and Effectuation: Toward a Theoretical
Shift from Economic Inevitability to Entrepreneurial Contingency. *The
Academy of Management Review, 26*(2), 243–263. https://doi.org/10.2307/
259121.

Sarasvathy, S. D. (2009). *Effectuation: Elements of Entrepreneurial Expertise*.
Edward Elgar.

Sarasvathy, S. D. (2021). Even-If: Sufficient, Yet Unnecessary Conditions for
Worldmaking. *Organization Theory, 2*(2), 26317877211005785. https://doi
.org/10.1177/26317877211005785.

Saward, M. (2021). *Democratic Design*. Oxford University Press.

Sayeed, O. B., & Gazdar, M. K. (2003). Intrapreneurship: Assessing and
Defining Attributes of Intrapreneurs. *The Journal of Entrepreneurship, 12*
(1), 75–89. https://doi.org/10.1177/097135570301200104.

Sayre, E. C., & Irving, P. W. (2015). Brief, Embedded, Spontaneous
Metacognitive Talk Indicates Thinking Like a Physicist. *Physical Review*

Special Topics – Physics Education Research, 11(2), 020121. https://doi.org/10.1103/PhysRevSTPER.11.020121.

Scherer, R., Siddiq, F., & Sánchez Viveros, B. (2019). The Cognitive Benefits of Learning Computer Programming: A Meta-Analysis of Transfer Effects. *Journal of Educational Psychology, 111*(5), 764–792. https://doi.org/10.1037/edu0000314.

Schroyer, T. (1984). On Finalization in Science. *Theory and Society, 13*(5), 715–723.

Schweitzer, J., Groeger, L., & Sobel, L. (2016). The Design Thinking Mindset: An Assessment of What We Know and What We See in Practice. *Journal of Design, Business & Society, 2*(1), 71–94. https://doi.org/10.1386/dbs.2.1.71_1.

Seiler, J. H., & Kowalsky, M. (2011). Systems Thinking Evidence from Colleges of Business and their Universities. *American Journal of Business Education (AJBE), 4*(3), Article 3. https://doi.org/10.19030/ajbe.v4i3.4113.

Seixas, P. (2017). A Model of Historical Thinking. *Educational Philosophy and Theory, 49*(6), 593–605. https://doi.org/10.1080/00131857.2015.1101363.

Selby, C. C., & Woollard, J. (2014). Computational Thinking: The Developing Definition. *Proceedings of the 45th ACM Technical Symposium on Computer Science Education*, 1–6.

Sevian, H., & Talanquer, V. (2014). Rethinking Chemistry: A Learning Progression on Chemical Thinking. *Chemistry Education Research and Practice, 15*(1), 10–23. https://doi.org/10.1039/C3RP00111C.

Shin, N., Bowers, J., Roderick, S. et al. (2022). A Framework for Supporting Systems Thinking and Computational Thinking Through Constructing Models. *Instructional Science, 50*(6), 933–960. https://doi.org/10.1007/s11251-022-09590-9.

Shulman, L. S. (2005). Signature Pedagogies in the Professions. *Daedalus, 134*(3), 52–59.

Shumway, D. R., & Messer-Davidow, E. (1991). Disciplinarity: An Introduction. *Poetics Today, 12*(2), 201–225. https://doi.org/10.2307/1772850.

Shute, V. J. (1994). Learning Processes and Learning Outcomes. In T. Husén & T. N. Postlethwaite (Eds.), *The International Encyclopedia of Education* (2nd ed., pp. 3315–3325). Pergamon ; Elsevier Science.

Shute, V. J., Sun, C., & Asbell-Clarke, J. (2017). Demystifying Computational Thinking. *Educational Research Review, 22*, 142–158. https://doi.org/10.1016/j.edurev.2017.09.003.

Smart, J. C., Ethington, C. A., Umbach, P. D., & Rocconi, L. M. (2009). Faculty Emphases on Alternative Course-Specific Learning Outcomes in Holland's

Model Environments: The Role of Environmental Consistency. *Research in Higher Education, 50*(5), 483–501. https://doi.org/10.1007/s11162-009-9125-z.

Sneider, C., Stephenson, C., Schafer, B., & Flick, L. (2014). Computational Thinking in High School Science Classrooms: Exploring the Science 'Framework' and 'NGSS'. *Science Teacher, 81*(5), 53–59.

Sokol, A., Oget, D., Sonntag, M., & Khomenko, N. (2008). The Development of Inventive Thinking Skills in the Upper Secondary Language Classroom. *Thinking Skills and Creativity, 3*(1), 34–46. https://doi.org/10.1016/j.tsc.2008.03.001.

Speicher, S., Murray, A., & McGirt, E. (2022, March 9). *IDEO's CEO Is Applying Design Thinking to Find Balance in the Pandemic Era.* Fortune. https://fortune.com/2022/03/09/ideo-ceo-sandy-speicher-design-thinking-covid-pandemic/.

Spiller, C., Wolfgramm, R. M., Henry, E., & Pouwhare, R. (2020). Paradigm Warriors: Advancing a Radical Ecosystems View of Collective Leadership from an Indigenous Māori Perspective. *Human Relations, 73,* 516–543. https://doi.org/10.1177/0018726719893753.

Stacey, M., & Eckert, C. (2003). Against Ambiguity. *Computer Supported Cooperative Work, 12*(2), 153–183.

Stanovich, K. E., & West, R. F. (1997). Reasoning Independently of Prior Belief and Individual Differences in Actively Open-Minded Thinking. *Journal of Educational Psychology, 89*(2), 342–357. https://doi.org/10.1037/0022-0663.89.2.342.

Stave, K., & Hopper, M. (2007, August 29). What Constitutes Systems Thinking: A Proposed Taxonomy. *25th International Conference of the System Dynamics Society,* 1–24. https://digitalscholarship.unlv.edu/sea_fa c_articles/201.

Stearns, S. C. (2006). Evolutionary Thinking in the Medical Sciences. In *Encyclopedia of Life Sciences* (pp. 1–3). John Wiley & Son. www.wiley .com/en-gb/Encyclopedia+of+Life+Sciences%2C+26+Volume+Set-p-9780470066515.

Sternberg, R. J. (1996). What is Mathematical Thinking? In R. J. Sternberg & T. Ben-Zeev (Eds.), *The Nature of Mathematical Thinking* (pp. 303–318). Routledge.

Sternberg, R. J. (2020). Critical Thinking in STEM Disciplines. In R. J. Sternberg & D. F. Halpern (Eds.), *Critical Thinking in Psychology* (2nd ed., pp. 309–327). Cambridge University Press. https://doi.org/10.1017/9781108684354.014.

Sternberg, R. J., & Ben-Zeev, T. (Eds.). (1996). *The Nature of Mathematical Thinking*. Routledge.

Stiling, P. (1994). What Do Ecologists Do? *Bulletin of the Ecological Society of America, 75*(2), 116–121.

Strober, M. H. (2006). Habits of the Mind: Challenges for Multidisciplinary Engagement. *Social Epistemology, 20*(3–4), 315–331. https://doi.org/10.1080/02691720600847324.

Strober, M. H. (2011). *Interdisciplinary Conversations: Challenging Habits of Thought*. Stanford University Press.

Sullivan, G. (2001). Artistic Thinking as Transcognitive Practice: A Reconciliation of the Process-Product Dichotomy. *Visual Arts Research, 27*(1), 2–12.

Suzuki, D. G. (2021). Homology Thinking Reconciles the Conceptual Conflict between Typological and Population Thinking. *Biology & Philosophy, 36*(2), 23. https://doi.org/10.1007/s10539-021-09800-7.

Tank, A. (2020, December 18). *This One Style of Thinking Helps My Team Solve Problems More Creatively*. Fast. www.fastcompany.com/90587741/how-my-company-uses-systems-thinking-to-solve-problems-faster.

Tanner, C. A. (2006). Thinking Like a Nurse: A Research-Based Model of Clinical Judgment in Nursing. *Journal of Nursing Education, 45*(6), 204–211. https://doi.org/10.3928/01484834-20060601-04.

Tedre, M., & Denning, P. J. (2022). Computational Thinking: A Professional and Historical Perspective. In A. Yadav & U. D. Berthelsen (Eds.), *Computational Thinking in Education: A Pedagogical Perspective* (pp. 1–17). Routledge. www.taylorfrancis.com/chapters/edit/10.4324/9781003102991-1/computational-thinking-matti-tedre-peter-denning.

Tett, G. (2021). *Anthro-Vision: A New Way to See in Business and Life*. Simon and Schuster.

Tollefsen, C. (2020). What Is 'Good Science'? In M. Bertolaso & F. Sterpetti (Eds.), *A Critical Reflection on Automated Science: Will Science Remain Human?* (pp. 279–292). Springer International Publishing. https://doi.org/10.1007/978-3-030-25001-0_14.

Treffinger, D. J., Isaksen, S. G., & Stead-Dorval, K. B. (2006). *Creative Problem Solving: An Introduction*. Prufrock Press.

UK Government Office for Science. (2022). *Systems Thinking: An Introductory Toolkit for Civil Servants*. UK Government Office for Science. www.gov.uk/government/publications/systems-thinking-for-civil-servants.

United Nations Development Programme. (2017). *Design Thinking | United Nations Development Programme*. UNDP. www.undp.org/arab-states/publications/design-thinking.

Valerio, A., Parton, B., & Robb, A. (2014). *Entrepreneurship Education and Training Programs around the World*. International Bank for Reconstruction and Development / The World Bank. https://documents1.worldbank.org/cur ated/en/237611468151500808/pdf/Entrepreneurship-education-and-train ing-programs-around-the-world-dimensions-for-success.pdf

Varadarajan, A. (2019). *Uncovering the Link Between Effectuation and Design Thinking in Early Stage Startups* [Master's Programme in International Design Business Management (IDBM), Aalto University]. https://aaltodoc .aalto.fi/bitstream/handle/123456789/42688/master_Varadarajan_Adithya_ 2020.pdf?sequence=1&isAllowed=y.

Vermaas, P. (2016). A Logical Critique of the Expert Position in Design Research: Beyond Expert Justification of Design Methods and Towards Empirical Validation. *Design Science, 2*, e7 (23 pages). https://doi.org/ 10.1017/dsj.2016.6.

Waks, S., Trotskovsky, E., Sabag, N., & Hazzam, O. (2011). Engineering Thinking: The Expert's Perspective. *International Journal of Engineering Education, 27*, 838–851.

Warton, D. I., Foster, S. D., De'ath, G., Stoklosa, J., & Dunstan, P. K. (2015). Model-Based Thinking for Community Ecology. *Plant Ecology, 216*(5), 669–682. https://doi.org/10.1007/s11258-014-0366-3.

Webster, P. R. (1990). Creativity as Creative Thinking. *Music Educators Journal, 76*(9), 22–28. https://doi.org/10.2307/3401073.

Wegerif, R. (2007). *Dialogic Education and Technology: Expanding the Space of Learning*. Springer. https://link.springer.com/book/10.1007/978-0-387-71142-3.

Wegerif, R., Li, L., & Kaufman, J. C. (Eds.). (2015). *The Routledge International Handbook of Research on Teaching Thinking*. Routledge.

Weintrop, D., Beheshti, E., Horn, M. et al. (2016). Defining Computational Thinking for Mathematics and Science Classrooms. *Journal of Science Education and Technology, 25*(1), 127–147. https://doi.org/10.1007/ s10956-015-9581-5.

Wiesche, M., Leifer, L., Uebernickel, F. et al. (2018). *Teaching Innovation in Interdisciplinary Environments: Toward a Design Thinking Syllabus*. AIS SIGED International Conference on Information Systems Education and Research. www.alexandria.unisg.ch/255309/.

Wild, C. J., & Pfannkuch, M. (1999). Statistical Thinking in Empirical Enquiry. *International Statistical Review, 67*(3), 223–248. https://doi.org/10.1111/ j.1751-5823.1999.tb00442.x.

Wilensky, U., & Resnick, M. (1999). Thinking in Levels: A Dynamic Systems Approach to Making Sense of the World. *Journal of Science Education and Technology, 8*(1), 3–19. https://doi.org/10.1023/A:1009421303064.

Willingham, D. T. (2007). Critical Thinking: Why Is It So Hard to Teach? *American Educator, 31*, 8–19.

Willingham, D. T. (2019). Occasional Paper Series: How to Teach Critical Thinking. *Education: Future Frontiers, State of New South Wales (Department of Education)*, 1–17.

Wineburg, S. (2010). Historical Thinking and Other Unnatural Acts. *Phi Delta Kappan, 92*(4), 81–94. https://doi.org/10.1177/003172171009200420.

Wing, J. M. (2006). Computational Thinking. *Communications of the ACM, 49* (3), 33–35. https://doi.org/10.1145/1118178.1118215.

Wing, J. M. (2008). Computational Thinking and Thinking about Computing. *Philosophical Transactions of the Royal Society A: Mathematical, Physical and Engineering Sciences, 366*(1881), 3717–3725. https://doi.org/10.1098/rsta.2008.0118.

Wittgenstein, L. (1968). *Philosophical Investigations* (Third ed.). Basil Blackwell.

Wrigley, C., Mosely, G., & Mosely, M. (2021). Defining Military Design Thinking: An Extensive, Critical Literature Review. *She Ji: The Journal of Design, Economics, and Innovation, 7*(1), 104–143. https://doi.org/10.1016/j.sheji.2020.12.002.

Wrigley, C., Mosely, G., & Tomitsch, M. (2018). Design Thinking Education: A Comparison of Massive Open Online Courses. *She Ji: The Journal of Design, Economics, and Innovation, 4*(3), 275–292. https://doi.org/10.1016/j.sheji.2018.06.002.

Wrigley, C., Nusem, E., & Straker, K. (2020). Implementing Design Thinking: Understanding Organizational Conditions. *California Management Review, 62*(2), 125–143. https://doi.org/10.1177/0008125619897606.

Wrigley, C., & Straker, K. (2017). Design Thinking Pedagogy: The Educational Design Ladder. *Innovations in Education and Teaching International, 54*(4), 374–385. https://doi.org/10.1080/14703297.2015.1108214.

Acknowledgements

In working on this project, I benefitted from opportunities to present and discuss my ideas at seminars with the University of Cambridge's Engineering Design Centre and Digital Education Futures Initiative, the University of Strathclyde's Department of Design, Manufacturing & Engineering Management, and Technical University of Delft's Faculties of Industrial Design Engineering and Technology, Policy and Management. Background work on bibliometric analysis and visualisation was supported by Owen Roberson and Niamh Malin. In addition to receiving helpful comments from three reviewers, I consulted with (in approximate chronological order) Esdras Paravizo, John Clarkson, Simon Peyton Jones, Alan Blackwell, David Good, Rupert Wegerif, Matthew Grimes, Peter Denning, Matti Tedre, Daniel Willingham, Bo Christensen, Linden Ball, Philip Cash, Emilie Colker, James Higgs, Lucy Kimbell, Paul Ingram, Sarah Woods, Lotta Hassi, Andy Dong, Lyn English and Pieter Vandekerckhove. I am grateful to all of them for their time discussing such a wide-ranging project and for directing me to relevant work that I would otherwise have overlooked. Finally, I would like to thank my parents for shaping how I see the world, orient toward it and act upon it.

Cambridge Elements ☰

Creativity and Imagination

Anna Abraham
University of Georgia, USA

Anna Abraham, Ph.D. is the E. Paul Torrance Professor at the University of Georgia, USA. Her notable publications include *The Neuroscience of Creativity* (2018, Cambridge University Press) and the edited volume, *The Cambridge Handbook of the Imagination* (2020).

About the Series

Cambridge Elements in Creativity and Imagination publishes original perspectives and insightful reviews of empirical research, methods, theories, or applications in the vast fields of creativity and the imagination. The series is particularly focused on showcasing novel, necessary and neglected perspectives.

Cambridge Elements $\equiv$

Creativity and Imagination

Elements in the Series

A full series listing is available at: www.cambridge.org/ECAI

Printed in the United States
by Baker & Taylor Publisher Services